The Coming

American Apocalypse

By Kim Wetteland

Pecan Grove Publishing
A division of Pecan Grove, LLC

Pecan Grove Publishing
www.pecangrovepublishing.com

Copyright © 2015, Kim Wetteland

All rights reserved, including the right to reproduce this book or portions thereof in any form whatsoever. All requests for reproduction must be made in writing to Pecan Grove Publishing, Rights Department, P.O. Box 5093, Woodridge, IL, 60517 or by email at permissions@pecangrovepublishing.com.

First edition, January, 2015

For information about bulk purchase and non-profit organization discounts, please contact Pecan Grove Publishing by email at npo@pecangrovepublishing.com, or visit our web site at www.pecangrovepublishing.com for more information.

Unless otherwise attributed, Scripture taken from the New King James Version®. Copyright © 1982 by Thomas Nelson. Used by permission. All rights reserved.

Cover design by Richard O. Ike.

Printed in the United States of America

10 9 8 7 6 5 4 3 2 1

ISBN 978-1-68128-000-4 (Print)
ISBN 978-1-68128-001-1 (Kindle)

Table of Contents

Introduction 1
Chapter One – The Vision 5
Chapter Two – When Liberty Crumbles 11
Chapter Three – Did George Washington See America's Future? 19
Chapter Four – Leaders Who Lead 25
Chapter Five – Can America Be Spared? 35
Chapter Six – The Church's Last Call 51
Chapter Seven – Restoring Our Influence 57
Chapter Eight – Ferguson, a Wake-Up Call 71
Chapter Nine – Dining with Zacchaeus 77
Chapter Ten – Freedom is Never Free 85
Chapter Eleven – The Face of Genuine Revival 97
Chapter Twelve – Share Your Story 109
Chapter Thirteen – Covert Affairs 117

Dedication

LeRoy A. Wetteland
U.S. Navy CPO, WWII
A True American Hero
1920 - 2003

"The day is coming, Kim, when the hardworking men of America won't be able to make a living and feed their families. Blood will fill the streets of America and fires will burn in every city! Corrupt judges and politicians will be shot. I won't be alive when this happens. I pray to God that you do not see this in your lifetime!"

LeRoy A. Wetteland, U.S. Navy CPO, WWII

The preceding quote is from my father, LeRoy A. Wetteland, U.S. Navy CPO WWII – a true American hero, to whom I owe my life and dedicate this book. A simple, common-sense hardworking man, my father, like everyone else in his generation, kept his word to all, demonstrated genuine honor, bravely served his country, and left a legacy of freedom that all of us have a responsibility to maintain.

As a young boy, I heard my dad's stories of war and The Great Depression hundreds of times. Looking back as an adult, I often wonder if my father possessed uncanny, prophetic insight into America's future.

My deepest, heartfelt prayer is that my father's heroic service, along with the vision and message of this book, do not fall upon deaf ears. For I truly believe the contents of this book comprise America's final warning, and the Church's Last Call.

Kim A. Wetteland
Missionary/Evangelist

Introduction

Twenty-two years ago, in a riveting open vision, I witnessed the total collapse of the greatest nation on earth – the United States of America. Currently, America is in a meltdown. Left-wing extremist judges autonomously overturn the majority votes of hardworking, taxpaying citizens. The Bible is becoming the new *"hate speech."* Pastors and Christian leaders are facing jail time for refusing to perform homosexual marriages as our religious liberties and free-speech rights face unprecedented attack. Rioting, looting, raging fires, and anarchy are beginning to spill into the streets of our nation's cities. And ISIS has threatened to raise their flag over our nation's capitol. America is spinning out of control!

I wrote this book because I believe there is still hope for America. Our nation need not collapse. Although our government is incapable of stopping America from falling off the cliff its racing towards and plunging headlong into the valley of an irreparable apocalypse – you, as a pastor, leader, businessman or woman, dad, mom, teenager, or average citizen; have all the qualities and abilities necessary to lead America back to the God of its Founding Fathers and spare our nation from calamity.

In this book you will learn what made America the most prosperous nation in the world and discover three shocking factors that were common in every great empire just prior to its total collapse – that currently are part of today's American culture. Most importantly, you will understand why you, and not government, have the power to change America's future. With step-by-step examples, this book will show you exactly what to do.

As a pastor or leader, you will learn how to influence your Community, Civic, State, and national political leaders, win them to your side, and lead them to Christ. You will discover how to plan, implement, and carry out a *"Covert Mission"* – allowing you to win hundreds of people to Christ inside of every local business within your municipality, double the size of your church congregations, and gain your community's respect. You will acquire key leadership abilities and learn how to pastor a church so Christ will respond to your obedience by sending revival to your community. By understanding how to implement the "keys" needed to change your communities, you will foster change in America from the grass roots level.

As a businessman or woman, you will learn how to influence your coworkers and supervisors, unite them to your team, and gain their favor. You will acquire the top-secret skills necessary to function in today's highly competitive job market, ethically climb the corporate ladder, and succeed without compromising your faith and values. Most importantly, however, you will learn how to lead people to Christ in the workplace without losing your job and advance change in America by impacting your work environment.

So let's journey through this book together and discover what fostered the success of the greatest nation on earth and find out where America took a wrong turn in the road and began to travel down the exact same paths that were previously taken by every great empire that no longer exists. But most of all let's discover how you can improve your status in life, make a difference in your community, and impact America's future for the sake of righteousness. So, let's turn the page, enter Chapter One, and find out what happened on a cold blustery day in Des Moines, Iowa, on March 6, 1993.

Chapter One
The Vision

Saturday, March 6, 1993 was a cold, blustery winter day in Des Moines, Iowa. The sun was shining, and yet, there was a bone-chilling nip in the air. My parents were visiting from their hometown of Aurora, Illinois. Two days earlier, our entire family celebrated my youngest daughter's fourth birthday. The time we shared together was priceless!

After finishing a hearty breakfast at the Village Inn Restaurant in West Des Moines, Iowa, my parents, along with my wife and four daughters, drove to the Valley West Mall for a few hours of shopping. Needing to organize some last-minute details for Sunday's church service, I stepped into my car and headed for the office. Everything seemed normal as I left the parking lot of the Village Inn Restaurant. I had no idea that my life was about to change, forever.

What's Happening to America?
Suddenly, to my right there was a huge explosion! On my left every building was on fire. Rioting, looting, murder, and mayhem filled the streets of America. Hard-working dads and moms, along with their teenagers and children were injured,

covered with blood, and walking the streets in a daze trying to process what had happened.

People were running, searching, screaming the names of their relatives, and turning over pieces of rubble hoping to find someone alive.

Police, Fire, and EMT's were overwhelmed by the carnage. Hospital emergency staff had to choose whom to save and whom to let die. Grocery store shelves were empty, unemployment skyrocketed, the U.S. Dollar crashed, and the financial markets dropped thousands of points in one day. The president declared a Nationwide State of Emergency, dispatched the National Guard, and instituted martial law. What was going on? What happened? How did this occur?

What Am I Seeing?
As I blinked my eyes and dried my tears, drivers in other vehicles began blowing their horns and yelling at me to move. I had no idea that I stopped my vehicle in the middle of 22nd Street and was blocking traffic. I pulled my car to the side of the road, parked, and began to cry hysterically.

What was I seeing? I blinked my eyes again, only to discover that I was having an open vision regarding the future of the United States of America. How could this be? I had heard of people having open visions, but did not really know if something like this was even possible.

Like viewing a high-tech Hollywood production on a large screen HDTV, the fires continued to burn before my eyes in sordid, living color. I watched in utter horror! Explosions were everywhere. Fear filled the streets and people were running for their lives. Mothers, with grief-filled eyes, stepped over dismembered body parts, frantically searching for any sign of life that may ignite some hope that their child was still alive. Chaos was everywhere!

America's Cities Are Burning!
As I pondered the vision, the scenery began to flash from city to city. New York, Denver, Boston, Chicago, Atlanta, Los Angeles, Phoenix, and Dallas: Every major city in America was engulfed in flames. Hundreds of fires were burning everywhere!

I recalled David Wilkerson's vision of 1,000 fires burning in New York City alone. Crime, mayhem, and lawlessness filled the streets of every major city in the United States of America! How could this happen to my country? Is this a terrorist attack? Why is God showing me this? Again, I began to sob without control.

With no warning, the scenery abruptly shifted to the White House in our nation's Capital. While peering into the oval office of the U.S. Presidency, a country church-type building was sitting on top of a large, hardwood negotiation table where members of the President's cabinet hashed out decisions for America's future. Waiting with anticipation regarding what I was about to see, the vision, unexpectedly, ended.

Don't Pray for Me! Pray for America!
Trying to dry my tears was futile. I had just witnessed the future destruction of my country and could not stop weeping. A passerby knocked on the window of my car and asked if I was

okay. I tried to speak, but was unable to communicate. I just kept crying.

I don't remember if this individual was a man or a woman, but they were very kindhearted and prayed for me. I tried to scream, "Don't pray for me! Pray for America!" But I could not speak. I was sobbing so profusely that the words I tried to utter refused to come out of my mouth. The passerby, who comforted me and prayed, went on their way.

The Collapse of America is Coming

Dazed and astonished, I continued to cry until the front of my shirt was soaked with tears! Before I was able to gather my wits and collect my thoughts, the crystal-clear voice of the Lord began to resonate inside my spirit:

> *"Unless genuine revival returns to the United States, everything you just saw in this vision will happen in America.*
>
> *Hundreds of fires will burn every major U.S. city to the ground. Numerous bombs will explode throughout the country. Crime, rioting, looting, and murder will assail from coast to coast. Hatred, racism, and vicious acts of terrorism will strike with such sudden force, that even the FBI will be caught completely off guard. America will be brought to its knees!*
>
> *The U.S. Dollar will crash, unemployment will skyrocket, the price of food will soar, and grocery stores will be empty.*
>
> *Banks will close their doors as hard-working dads and moms try to withdraw money that is no longer available.*

> *Wall Street investments will drop thousands of points in one day! Police, fire, and rescue workers will be overwhelmed. The National Guard will patrol the streets with military vehicles and your President will institute martial law as China replaces the United States as the world's new superpower!"*

America Must Be Warned!

For a moment there was a pause of silence which seemed to last an eternity. At this point, I could almost feel passionate emotion from the heart of God as He pleaded:

> *"You must understand the mystery and the meaning of the country church-type building sitting on the negotiation table in the oval office of the U.S. Presidency. The day will come when legislation will pour out of Washington in Satan's attempt to cripple and stop the American Church!"*

And then, with the most authoritative command I have ever heard in my life, deep within my spirit the Lord's voice thundered, *"Go wake up America and the American church!"*

I was stunned. Shaking, quivering, and weeping, I was unable to continue on to my office. I drove home and sat on the edge of my bed waiting for my wife to arrive home from shopping.

When Cherie entered the bedroom I tried to tell her what had just happened, but again, I was not able to speak. Both of us sobbed profusely as we tightly embraced one another. When I was finally able to tell my wife what had occurred, she wept, too. Both of us instinctively knew that our nation was in grave danger. In order to avert a horrific apocalypse, I had to awaken America, and the American church.

Chapter Two
When Liberty Crumbles

Twenty-two years have passed since I had this vision and initially wrote the contents in my journal. During this time, the details of this experience have only been shared with a few family members and close friends. I never had a sense of urgency, or any hint of direction from the Lord, to publicly share this vision through the various avenues of the media or a book, until now. Conditions in the United States and the world have reached a point, where, if something is not done immediately, America will fall off the cliff it is racing towards and plunge into the valley of an irreparable apocalypse!

America Is In Crisis

As Christians, we have become so drunk with the wine of pointing our fingers at one another's doctrinal differences that we are blind to the needs in our own communities. Like the priest and the Levite, we pass by the suffering people in our Jericho community streets, leaving God no option other than to use Samaritans (government programs) to care for the needy. Then we criticize the politicians whom we elected, and cry socialism, while we sit in our pews and demand God to bring people into our declining church services from the north, south, east, and west. Interesting, I thought Jesus said that we are to go into our communities and heal the brokenhearted, feed the hungry, clothe the poor, love the sinners, and BRING them in! Having lost touch with God, reality, and common sense, we join hands in prayer imploring Christ to do what He commanded us to do while we wear rose-colored glasses and pretend the homegrown jihadists, currently living in our nation, do not really possess the level of organization needed to reign terror in our cities from coast to coast. We are facing a serious crisis!

In 1942, Jan Karski warned of a holocaust that was going to kill millions of Jews. He pleaded with the United States and Great Britain to do something about it. But no one would listen. No one believed him!

I'm concerned that we may be just years away from hundreds of fires burning in each of our major American cities, with the power grids shut down, and our corporate and governmental computer systems under the control of skillful jihadist hackers whom we educated at our own universities. We are at the very doorstep of terror reigning down on America! The questions are, will anyone heed this book's warning, take a stand, and do something?

Terrorism, Anger, Disease

The Muslim terrorist regime of ISIS is presently on the verge of conquering numerous major cities in the tumultuous Middle East. Our current American president, Barack Obama, remains firm in his policy of having "no boots on the ground" even though military experts and generals warn that ISIS cannot be defeated with air strikes alone. While American politicians continue the debate of trying to figure out who will pull their pants up and be a real leader, ISIS continues to raise their flag over newly, overthrown cities in an openly declared quest to establish a global caliphate. A *caliphate* is an Islamic state. It's led by a *caliph*, who is a political and religious leader who is a successor (caliph) to the Islamic prophet Muhammad. His power and authority is absolute. ISIS is resolute in their pursuit of worldwide domination. Their stated goal is to raise the ISIS flag over the White House. And make no mistake about it; they are educated, well organized, and willing to die for their agenda!

In Ferguson, Missouri citizens and civil rights groups are in an uproar over the shooting of a black teenager by a Caucasian police officer. Rioting, pain, and confusion are beginning to fill America's streets.

The deadly Ebola virus is killing thousands of innocent, hard-working moms, dads, and children in West Africa. Americans tremble in fear as Ebola has made its way across the great Atlantic Ocean on a routine commercial airline flight, arrived in a Dallas hospital, and killed Thomas Eric Duncan, a soft spoken, kind-hearted man. Two heroic nurses, Nina Pham and Amber Vinson, fell ill with this terrible virus while caring for Mr. Duncan. Although Nina and Amber both fully recovered, many are disenchanted over a consensus of lack in American leadership. Dr. Thomas Frieden is replaced as leader of the Center for Disease Control due to a national outcry for his resignation. Scientists and experts in the field of infectious disease control differ widely in their approach to handling deadly viruses like Ebola. America is confused!

What Happened To Freedom?

Religious liberties are under attack in an unprecedented manner. In 2014, Kendra Turner, an 18-year-old student from the Dyer County High School in Newbern, Tennessee, was punished with an in-school suspension for saying the words "bless you," after she heard another student sneeze. A fellow classmate sent a local Tennessee television station a photo taken inside the teacher's classroom showing a list of banned words. Among the censored words are "dumb," "stupid," and "bless you." A school official told a FOX News reporter there was no ban on the words "bless you" even though the classroom photograph proves otherwise. If it were not for the fact that this story is true, most people with common sense would think this must be some kind of joke authored by a comic script team of writers for Jay Leno. But this is no joke! Jailed as hostages behind the prison bars of a broken, public school system, our children are being indoctrinated by a radical group of elite educators who openly and brazenly shame and punish those students who demonstrate acts of noncompliance by refusing to drink their politically correct poison.

What was once known as free speech is now considered "hate speech" or a "hate crime" for a Christian or a pastor to denounce fornication, adultery, homosexuality, and same-sex marriage as sinful inappropriate lifestyle choices that will result in much pain. Gone are the days when an individual is allowed to freely agree or disagree with an issue in the forum of public opinion. This, however, is not the case for individuals who are gay, lesbian, transsexual, or for a Muslim who desires to govern a select American community with Sharia law. Then, tolerance is demanded by the politically correct and enforced by activist judges who practice intolerance against anyone who believes in or proclaims the Gospel message of Jesus Christ. Wake up! We are living in a post-Christian American era! We must take a firm stand, now!

In December of 2013, a Colorado baker was ordered by a judge to either bake cakes for gay weddings or face fines. Jack Phillips, the owner of Masterpiece Cakeshop, was told to "cease and desist from discriminating" against gay couples. As a committed Christian, Phillips must be wondering why the nation he loves is trying to intimidate him into violating his personal faith and beliefs. The gay couple could purchase a cake from any number of other bakeries. What possible motive could there be for singling out this one man?

New Mexico's Supreme Court ruled in August of 2013 that two Christian photographers who declined to photograph a same-sex union violated the state's Human Rights Act. One justice said photographers Elaine and Jonathan Huguenin were "compelled by law to compromise the very religious beliefs that inspire their lives." Can you believe that a judge actually demanded a Christian couple to compromise their religious beliefs or face fines and or possible imprisonment?

What's Happening to America?
In October of 2014 the city of Houston issued subpoenas demanding a group of pastors turn over any sermons dealing with homosexuality, gender identity, or comments regarding Annise Parker, the city's first openly lesbian mayor. Those ministers who fail to comply were told they could be held in contempt of court. The subpoenas were the latest incident in an ongoing battle over Houston's new non-discrimination ordinance. The law, among other things, would allow men to use the ladies room and vice versa. More than 400 Houston area

churches opposed this law that the city Council approved in June.

After opponents of the bathroom bill filed a lawsuit, the city's attorneys responded by issuing the subpoenas against the pastors of churches who voiced their opposition to the new law. This is exactly what Todd Starnes described in his book, *God Less America*. He predicted that the government would one day try to silence American pastors, and that under the guise of "tolerance and diversity," elected officials would attempt to deconstruct religious liberty and segregate free speech.

On October 15th, Houston Mayor Annise Parker backed down from the subpoenas the city of Houston had issued to the pastors. After a nationwide outcry the Mayor told a Houston radio station that she had changed her mind.

Separation of Church and State

The modern misnomer of "separation of church and state," which is commonly accepted and taught in our educational institutions as the original intent of our forefathers, cannot be found anywhere in the United States Constitution because it is not there. The whole idea of "separation of church and state" came from a statement made by Thomas Jefferson in a letter he wrote to the Danbury Baptists in defense of his position that a wall of separation must be established within our legislative system in order to protect the church from the possible intrusion and tyranny by a government that oversteps its boundaries. Please read the quote from Jefferson's letter.

> *"Believing with you that religion is a matter which lies solely between man and his God; that he owes account*

When Liberty Crumbles

to none other for his faith or his worship; that the legislative powers of government reach actions only and not opinions, I contemplate with sovereign reverence that act of the whole American people which declared that their legislature should 'make no law respecting an establishment of religion or prohibiting the free exercise thereof,' thus building a wall of separation between Church and State."

Jefferson clearly understood the need to build a wall of legislative separation that would protect the religious liberties, freedoms, and rights of American citizens from government intrusion into what the Church can believe and preach. Thomas Jefferson did not say there needs to be a wall of separation to protect the government from the Church. He declared there needs to be a wall of separation to protect the Church from our government! Jefferson and our founding fathers understood that if our liberties crumble, our nation would collapse.

Chapter Three
Did George Washington See America's Future?

I truly believe there is hope for the United States of America. God is not finished with our great nation. With America on the verge of an apocalypse this country has never witnessed, something must be done now. There is an urgency within my spirit to sound an alarm! I am not the only person to have experienced a divine encounter with God regarding America's future. Many have had a similar experience.

One such account came from a very famous American, whose insight into our nation's future, used to be standard reading material in our public schools. Possibly you have heard of this great pioneer. He is the father of our country and the first president of the United States of America, George Washington.

George Washington's Vision
This afternoon, as I was sitting at this table engaged in preparing a dispatch, something seemed to disturb me. Looking up, I beheld standing opposite me a singularly beautiful female. So astonished was I, for I had given strict orders not to be disturbed, that it was some

moments before I found language to inquire the cause of her presence. A second, a third and even a fourth time did I repeat my question, but received no answer from my mysterious visitor except a slight raising of her eyes.

By this time, I felt strange sensations spreading through me. I would have risen but the riveted gaze of the being before me rendered volition impossible. I assayed once more to address her, but my tongue had become useless, as though it had become paralyzed.

A new influence, mysterious, potent, irresistible, took possession of me. All I could do was to gaze steadily, vacantly at my unknown visitor. Gradually the surrounding atmosphere seemed as if it had become filled with sensations, and luminous. Everything about me seemed to rarefy, the mysterious visitor herself becoming more airy and yet more distinct to my sight than before. I now began to feel as one dying, or rather to experience the sensations which I have sometimes imagined accompany dissolution. I did not think, I did not reason, I did not move; all were alike impossible. I was only conscious of gazing fixedly, vacantly at my companion.

Presently I heard a voice saying, "Son of the Republic, look and learn," while at the same time my visitor extended her arm eastwardly. I now beheld a heavy white vapor at some distance rising fold upon fold. This gradually dissipated, and I looked upon a stranger scene. Before me lay spread out in one vast plain all the countries of the world — Europe, Asia, Africa and America. I saw rolling and tossing between Europe and America the billows of the Atlantic, and between Asia and America lay the Pacific.

Did George Washington See America's Future?

"Son of the Republic," said the same mysterious voice as before, "look and learn." At that moment, I beheld a dark, shadowy being, like an angel, standing or rather floating in mid-air, between Europe and America. Dipping water out of the ocean in the hollow of each hand, he sprinkled some upon America with his right hand, while with his left hand he cast some on Europe. Immediately a cloud raised from these countries, and joined in mid-ocean. For a while it remained stationary, and then moved slowly westward, until it enveloped America in its murky folds. Sharp flashes of lightning gleamed through it at intervals, and I heard the smothered groans and cries of the American people.

A second time the angel dipped water from the ocean, and sprinkled it out as before. The dark cloud was then drawn back to the ocean, in whose heaving billows it sank from view. A third time I heard the mysterious voice saying, "Son of the Republic, look and learn." I cast my eyes upon America and beheld villages and towns and cities springing up one after another until the whole land from the Atlantic to the Pacific was dotted with them.

Again, I heard the mysterious voice say, "Son of the Republic, the end of the century cometh, look and learn." At this the dark shadowy angel turned his face southward, and from Africa I saw an ill-omened specter approach our land. It flitted slowly over every town and city of the latter. The inhabitants presently set themselves in battle array against each other. As I continued looking I saw a bright angel, on whose brow rested a crown of light, on which was traced the word "Union," bearing the American flag which he placed between the divided nation, and said, "Remember ye are brethren." *Instantly, the inhabitants, casting from them their weapons became friends once more, and united around the National Standard.*

And again, I heard the mysterious voice saying, "Son of the Republic, look and learn." At this the dark, shadowy angel placed a trumpet to his mouth, and blew three distinct blasts; and taking water from the ocean, he sprinkled it upon Europe, Asia and Africa. Then my eyes beheld a fearful scene: From each of these countries arose thick, black clouds that were soon joined into one. Throughout this mass there gleamed a dark red light by which I saw hordes of armed men, who, moving with the cloud marched by land and sailed by sea to America. Our country was enveloped in this volume of cloud, and I saw these vast armies devastate the whole country and burn the villages, towns, and cities that I beheld springing up.

As my ears listened to the thundering of the cannon, clashing of sword, and the shouts and cries of millions in mortal combat, I heard again the mysterious voice saying, "Son of the Republic, look and learn." When the voice had ceased, the dark shadowy angel placed his trumpet once more to his mouth, and blew a long and fearful blast. Instantly a light as of a thousand suns shone down from above me, and pierced and broke into fragments the dark cloud which enveloped America. At the same moment, the angel upon whose head still shone the word Union, and who bore our national flag in one hand and a sword in the other, descended from the heavens attended by legions of white spirits. These immediately joined the inhabitants of America, who I

Did George Washington See America's Future?

perceived were will nigh overcome, but who immediately taking courage again, closed up their broken ranks and renewed the battle.

Again, amid the fearful noise of the conflict, I heard the mysterious voice saying, "Son of the Republic, look and learn." As the voice ceased, the shadowy angel for the last time dipped water from the ocean and sprinkled it upon America. Instantly the dark cloud rolled back, together with the armies it had brought, leaving the inhabitants of the land victorious!

Then once more, I beheld the villages, towns and cities springing up where I had seen them before, while the bright angel, planting the azure standard he had brought in the midst of them, cried with a loud voice: "While the stars remain, and the heavens send down dew upon the earth, so long shall the Union last." And taking from his brow the crown on which blazoned the word "Union," he placed it upon the Standard while the people, kneeling down, said, "Amen."

The scene instantly began to fade and dissolve, and I at last saw nothing but the rising, curling vapor I at first beheld. This also disappearing, I found myself once more gazing upon the mysterious visitor, who, in the same voice I had heard before, said, "Son of the Republic, what you have seen is thus interpreted: Three great perils will come upon the Republic. The most fearful is the third, but in this greatest conflict the whole world united shall not prevail against her. Let every child of the Republic learn to live for his God, his land and the Union." With these words the vision vanished, and I started from my seat and felt that I had seen a

The Coming American Apocalypse

vision wherein had been shown to me the birth, progress, and destiny of the United States.

http://www.ushistory.org/valleyforge/washington/vision.html

Chapter Four
Leaders Who Lead

I am neither a teacher nor an expert in the subject of end-time prophecy. All I know is that God, for whatever reason, decided to interrupt my peaceful day back in March of 1993 with an open vision regarding the future collapse of America. A plan was included with this vision, to avert a terrible apocalypse. Genuine revival must revisit America!

Webster defines revival as "...an act or instance of reviving, the state of being revived, or, the act or instance of bringing something back to life." According to Webster, the antonym or opposite of revival is "...death, expiration, and extinction."

Humility and Serving Needed
America is dying before our eyes! Our major cities, suburbs, and rural neighborhoods are in critical need of life. While our communities desperately need churches working together to bind up the brokenhearted, comfort the sick and bereaved, educate our teens, and feed the poor; far too much of the time we as leaders focus on minor doctrinal differences amongst one another which are of little or no consequence.

The disciples were engaged in an intense debate over which one of them would be the greatest. Jesus, perceiving their thoughts, placed a child in their midst and said, *"...whoever receives this little child in My name receives Me; and whoever receives Me receives Him who sent Me. For he who is least among you all will be great"* (Luke 9:48).

Jesus painted a powerful picture of humility and serving. If we link arms with our upcoming generation of adolescents or be the type of dads and moms who remain connected to their teens and raise a good family, we are living in the center of what Jesus coined as achieving greatness. Why? This is because our offspring are the future leaders of this nation. Investing quality time in our young people will allow us to impact their lives and shape the next generation of dads, moms, business owners, and community leaders; ensuring that our nation remains on course. Humility and serving are trademarks of *"Leaders Who Lead."*

He is not from Our Denomination

I truly believe the disciples bonded with Christ's message. They were elated! As part of the "in group" of their day and amongst the Who's Who of emerging religious leaders on a fast track to becoming famous, John had to make sure they remained exclusive. So with this ulterior motive in mind, he proclaimed, *"...Master, we saw someone casting out demons in Your name, and we forbade him because he does not follow with us"* (Luke 9:49).

John wanted to stop another minister from preaching the gospel because he was not a part of their group. Let me paraphrase John's thoughts. "Jesus, there is a pastor on the other side of town and he does not teach things the way we teach them. His customs are different and he belongs to a different denomination so we told him to stop!" But Jesus, patiently understanding that John's character had not yet caught up with his zeal, said to him, *"Do not forbid him, for he who is not against us is on our side"* *(Luke 9:50).*

Why do we spend so much of our focus centered on changing the beliefs of one another in order to make everyone just like us? Even Jesus understands that every Christian is not going to think and teach things in the exact same manner. Making room for differences amongst one another is a hallmark in Christ's teachings, is evidence of maturity, and is a character trait of being a *"Leader Who Leads."*

The Tale of Two Pastors

Several years ago, I was preaching for a very well-known pastor in one of America's larger metropolitan cities. This ministry was leading many people to Christ and doing a wonderful work. After the service the pastor and I enjoyed lunch in the privacy of his study. The meal was exquisite! While discussing how wonderfully God had touched the lives of people, out of the blue, this pastor began to speak critically of another minister who was the pastor of a church across the river on the opposite side of the city. Although I tried to point out some very good things about this other ministry, this pastor was adamant in his conviction that this other minister was a false teacher. Casually, I inquired if he had ever sat down with this other preacher or visited his church? With fire in his eyes this pastor said, "Why would I set foot on the property of another individual who is known to teach false doctrine?"

Several years later, you guessed it; the pastor across the river on the opposite side of this city invited me to speak in his church. As a missionary evangelist who has spoken in more than 600 local churches, conventions, and outdoor crusades worldwide, I have learned to value the inconsequential differences in our various independent, nondenominational, and denominational churches. So, I gladly accepted the invitation.

Similar to the church where I had spoken on the other side of the city two years earlier, the service in this assembly also was phenomenal. At the conclusion of my teaching, the pastor shared a simple, three-minute salvation message. Nearly 40 people responded to the invitation and walked to the altar to publicly surrender their lives to Christ.

After the service the pastor and I were in his office discussing the goodness of God, when out of the blue, this minister also began to speak in a demeaning manner of the same pastor that had spoken critically of him two years earlier. Both pastors were good men with biblically unblemished works in the same city. Although neither pastor had ever met or visited his colleague's church, both men accused the other of teaching false doctrine.

Time to Lay Pride Aside
Unfortunately, this scenario happens far too often among ministers from different denominational camps. How can we expect others to listen to us, when we as preachers, argue, fight, fuss, and bicker with one another? The time has come to put an end to all of this needless nitpicking and finger-pointing. Our churches and our nation are in a meltdown. And yet, the current crisis in America affords the Church its greatest opportunity ever. For, if we as leaders would dare to exercise the courage

needed to lay aside our pride, value our differences, and link hearts and arms to serve one another and our communities as a united army of compassion, we have within our grasp the ability to set this great nation back on course and avert a terrible apocalypse. According to Dr. Steve Vickers, "Having leaders without courage is worse than having no leaders at all."

The Apologists Need To Apologize

Far too numerous are the Christian apologists who need to apologize for slandering their own brethren. Like Diotrephes, who loved to be in charge of everything (3rd John vs. 9), we cleverly cover our prideful quest for celebrity status by claiming we are contending for the faith, standing up for the real truth, and exposing false teachers. In reality, these are just excuses to somehow justify our public slander of fellow comrades while we practice the skillful art of using the Bible to assassinate the character of other people and promote ourselves.

I cannot find any place in the Old or New Testaments that ordain an individual to a ministry of listening to every minuscule word of another preacher's recorded sermons under the magnifying glass of trying to find and expose false doctrine. Jesus warned of the danger and hypocrisy of focusing on the flaws in other people, saying, *"Why do you look at the speck of sawdust in your brother's eye and pay no attention to the plank in your own eye?" (Matthew 7:3).* Solomon referred to this self-ordained practice of extrospection as *sowing discord among the brethren (Proverbs 6:19),* which is included in the list of six things hated most by God and classified as an abomination!

Scripture offers a stern warning to us as leaders; *"But if you bite and devour one another, beware lest you be consumed by one another!" (Galatians 5:15).* As one who formerly persecuted Christians, Paul had firsthand knowledge of how searching for faults in the lives of other people bears the horrific fruit of the Church losing its place of influence in society while a nation forfeits its sovereign ability to command respect in the world. Like Jesus said, *"If a house is divided against itself, that house cannot stand" (Mark 3:25).*

Unity Is Valuing Our Differences

As Webster so clearly defined, *"Revival is the act or instance of bringing something back to life."* Our churches, cities, towns, rural America, and our nation desperately need revival! Revival is life! True revival, or life, cannot coexist in an atmosphere that is filled with arguing, strife, backbiting, finger-pointing, gossip, discord, and sectarianism. Jesus expects us, as His Body, to make room for differences in one another, to grow into mature believers, work together, and serve our communities.

As the Psalmist said, *"Behold, how good and how pleasant it is for brethren to dwell together in unity."* This is because unity is the place where God commands *"...the blessing, even life forevermore"* (Psalm 133:1, 3b). God decrees life, or revival, when there is harmony among the various denominational groups which comprise His Body, the Church. I believe God purposely ordained differences within His Church so that each of us would have to choose a life of pride, or humility, in order to work together. Jesus prayed that we would be one in the same way that He and the Father are one (John 17:21).

Wash One Another's Feet

In dramatic fashion, all of the Church's future leaders gathered for the grand finale of all Leadership Training Seminars. This was an invitation-only event with Jesus being the keynote speaker. Every disciple was there. Neither of them assessed or taught the Bible, precisely, in the same manner. Each of them possessed strong, differing opinions. Jesus knew that His greatest leadership challenge would be fought and won on the battlefield, of instilling within each apostle the wisdom needed to value the unique differences in one another, to always lay aside the enemy of pride, and to work together as a team.

The method that Christ chose to convey and impart truth is equally important as the message He proclaimed at this crucial Leadership Training Seminar. Instead of going to the platform and standing behind a podium, Jesus chose to be vulnerable, went down to where His disciples lived life, and gathered them into a small circle for close, one on one ministry. After removing His priestly garments of authority and changing into clothing worn by common servants, Jesus poured water into a basin and began to wash the feet of each leader; some of whom held differing, opposing viewpoints and struggled to get along with one another.

The actual teaching portion of this seminar was very brief. Jesus simply said, *"If I, then, your Lord and Teacher, have washed your feet, you also ought to wash one another's feet. For I have given you an example, that you should do as I have done to you"* (John 13:14-15).

Listen! This is Christ's model for how we as leaders are to treat one another. Jesus knew that when we, as pastors and leaders, wash the feet of other pastors and leaders with whom we differ, our hearts and eyes open so we may perceive our own pride, and value our need for one another.

Jesus never taught His leaders to simply get along with one another for the sake of unity. That approach is mere ecumenicalism, which in hundreds of years of trial and error, has proven to never bear fruit. Christ's approach, however, requires repentance, humility, and a willingness to serve one another.

When we as God's leaders in a community, find ourselves in disagreement, we are to serve each other and wash one another's feet! Our hearts will be exposed and open, not just to God, but to one another. Coming face to face with our own sin, shortcomings, and individual pride, God will then be free to work in each of our hearts to establish His love, respect, and appreciation for one another. Then, as a diverse, unified team of distinct churches, we may demonstrate cooperative leadership, serve the needs in our communities, refocus the course of our nation, and prevent a horrific apocalyptic ultimatum. Our nation will unify, when we as pastors and leaders, graduate from Christ's *Leadership Training Seminar* and begin to wash one another's feet!

Divided Churches – A Divided Nation!

The state of our country is contingent upon the condition of our churches. When those of us in Christ's Body, unify, our nation will unite! America currently is divided because our churches are divided. Genuine revival, on a nationwide scale, will only occur when we, as pastors and leaders, lay aside our pride and differing opinions, and purposely make the choice to serve each other, and to wash one another's feet. Make no mistake about it; the fate of America's future is at stake. Will we continue to fight, argue, and bicker with one another over inconsequential differences and face apocalypse due to our own self-centered behavior? Or, will all of us, together, choose to lay aside our pride and walk across the denominational aisles that divide us, wash one another's feet, and join forces to bind up the brokenhearted, feed the hungry, clothe the poor, mentor our teenagers, and serve our communities?

Laying aside our inconsequential differences, however, does not mean that we forsake the Cardinal truths of righteousness and begin to work with churches or denominations that reject Christ's deity, ordain and marry homosexuals, teach Unitarianism, promote other long-standing heresies, or are a part of the worldwide move to unite all the religions of man under one canopy. This is something we must never do! A clear line of separation must be drawn and maintained as no true disciple of Jesus Christ may participate in or unite with unrighteousness (2 Corinthians 6:14-16).

The future of our nation is hanging in the balance of the choices that we, as pastors and leaders, make. We need an insurgence of courageous, selfless-servant leaders to refocus our churches, and to advance our nation forward. We need *"Leaders Who Lead!"*

Chapter Five
Can America Be Spared?

History reveals that great nations rise and fall. The only thing remaining from the great Assyrian Empire, Babylonian Empire, and the Roman Empire, are a few remaining artifacts on display in modern museums. Why did these nations crumble? What lessons are revealed in history and what can we learn from the past? Will the United States of America follow in the footsteps of all the preceding superpowers and crumble in a pile of ashes? Or, can America somehow be spared from the plight of its own decadence?

The history of the world is the anthology of nations and sovereign empires that once prospered only to vanish into the sunset of an abyss. Why do nations degenerate and exit the world's stage? Time and again, history corroborates that a nation's moral condition and its character are key to its endurance and survival.

Common Attributes in Great Nations
Before we examine the common elements that contributed to the collapse of the world's great empires, let's take a look at six, vital attributes that can be found in all great nations.

1. A large, centralized population for productivity
First, a developed nation must have a large, centralized population situated near the production centers in order to fuel the economic engine and provide efficient production and supply capacities.

2. Abundance of resources and infinite production capacity
Secondly, a productive society involves an abundance of resources and the capacity to out-produce the needs of its population.

3. Conjoined government for infrastructure and protection
A thriving civilization must have a strong central government supported by appropriate taxation levels that are sufficient enough to provide protection for its citizens, but no more.

4. An ethical division of labor
An effective cooperation of labor must exist between corporations, business owners, and the generalized workforce.

5. Creativity for new product development and revenue generation
All great nations are born in an environment that fosters productivity, creativity, and innovative solutions. When citizens are liberated from excessive government control, a society is free to dream, pioneer, and achieve great things.

6. Religious framework and a moral foundation

An enduring civilization must have a religious, moral framework to foster unity, stability, and social cohesion. Historian Will Durant cites that "...there is no significant example in history, before our time, of a society successfully maintaining moral life without the aid of religion." History has demonstrated that when a nation moves away from its religious foundation and becomes morally corrupt, the society becomes volatile, and the nation moves towards collapse.

America's True Foundation

Today, many are attempting to rewrite history and allege that America has no biblical or Christian roots, and that our founding fathers were mainly deists, and not Christians. This ideology is not even remotely close to the historical truth!

In addition to their repudiation of the Bible's divine inspiration, deists deny the virgin birth and implicit deity of Christ. They believe a God exists, but that He is not directly involved in world affairs. Deism was not the belief system championed by our nation's founders. All of America's historical records and documentation affirm that an overwhelming consensus of our founding fathers were Christians who read the Bible and worshipped Jesus Christ.

According to Jim Bramlett, 52 of the 55 framers of the United States Constitution publicly affirmed they were Christians. A University of Houston study discovered that 34% of all our founding fathers' quotes came from the Bible, 60% of their citations were from men who used the Bible to form their conclusions, and a grand total of 94% of all the quotations from America's historic fathers cited the Bible, either directly or indirectly, as their basis for substance and truth. Most early Americans were Bible-believing Christians who drew upon their faith and biblical principles to construct the framing documents of our country.

James Madison, the chief architect of the U.S. Constitution, said, "We have staked the whole future of American civilization, not upon the power of government, far from it. We have staked the future of all of our political institutions upon the capacity of mankind for self-government; upon the capacity of each and all of us to govern ourselves, to control ourselves, to sustain ourselves according to the Ten Commandments of God."

Alexander Hamilton, who helped to ratify the Constitution, said, "I have carefully examined the evidence of the Christian religion, and if I was sitting as a juror upon its authenticity I would unhesitatingly give my verdict in its favor. I can prove its truth as clearly as any proposition ever submitted to the mind of man."

The famous American Revolutionary leader, Patrick Henry, said, "It cannot be emphasized too strongly or too often that this great nation was founded, not by religionists, but by Christians; not on religions, but on the gospel of Jesus Christ."

Our sixth president, John Quincy Adams, said, "The highest glory of the American Revolution was this: It connected in one indissoluble bond, the principles of civil government and the principles of Christianity."

Can America Be Spared?

And let's not forget the famous Thanksgiving Proclamation issued on October 3, 1789, by the father of our country and first president of the United States of America.

Washington's Thanksgiving Proclamation

"Whereas it is the duty of all Nations to acknowledge the providence of Almighty God, to obey his will, to be grateful for his benefits, and humbly to implore his protection and favor – and whereas both Houses of Congress have by their joint Committee requested me to recommend to the People of the United States a day of public thanksgiving and prayer to be observed by acknowledging with grateful hearts the many signal favors of Almighty God especially by affording them an opportunity peaceably to establish a form of government for their safety and happiness.

Now therefore I do recommend and assign Thursday the 26th day of November next to be devoted by the People of these States to the service of that great and glorious Being, who is the beneficent Author of all the good that was, that is, or that will be – That we may then all unite in rendering unto him our sincere and humble thanks – for his kind care and protection of the People of this Country previous to their becoming a Nation – for the signal and manifold mercies, and the favorable interpositions of his Providence which we experienced in the course and conclusion of the late war – for the great degree of tranquility, union, and plenty, which we have since enjoyed – for the peaceable and rational manner, in which we have been enabled to establish constitutions of government for our safety and happiness, and particularly the national one now lately instituted – for the civil and religious liberty with which we are blessed; and the means we have of acquiring and diffusing useful knowledge; and in general for all the great and various favors which he hath been pleased to confer upon us.

And also that we may then unite in most humbly offering our prayers and supplications to the great Lord and Ruler of Nations and beseech him to pardon our national and other transgressions – to enable us all, whether in public or private stations, to perform our several and relative duties properly and punctually – to render our national government a blessing to all the people, by constantly being a Government of wise, just, and constitutional laws, discreetly and faithfully executed and obeyed – to protect and guide all Sovereigns and Nations (especially such as have shewn kindness unto us) and to bless them with good government, peace, and concord – To promote the knowledge and practice of true religion and virtue, and the increase of science among them and us – and generally to grant unto all Mankind such a degree of temporal prosperity as he alone knows to be best."

Given under my hand at the City of New York the third day of October in the year of our Lord, 1789. George Washington.

Were Our Founders Deists Or Christians?
Clearly, the United States of America was founded by a majority of Christians, and upon Christian and biblical principles of law and morality. True, a few of America's founders were not Bible-believing Christians, and yet, they still espoused a biblical worldview.

Can America Be Spared?

There are many who cite Thomas Jefferson as an advocate of deism. Although Jefferson may not have been an evangelical Christian, consider his warning that applies to all.

"God gave us life and gave us liberty. And can the liberties of a nation be thought secure when we have removed their only firm basis, a conviction in the minds of the people that these liberties are of the Gift of God? That they are not to be violated but with His wrath? Indeed, I tremble for my country when I reflect that God is just; that His justice cannot sleep forever."

The great Benjamin Franklin, who also is considered to be a deist, galvanized the deadlocked Constitutional Convention in 1787 with the following address to the caucus president, George Washington.

"We have not hitherto once thought of humbly applying to the Father of Lights to illuminate our understanding. In the beginning of the contest with Great Britain, when we were sensible to danger, we had daily prayers in this room for divine protection. Our prayers, sir, were heard, and they were graciously answered. Do we imagine that we no longer need His assistance? I have lived, sir, a long time, and the longer I live, the more convincing proofs I see of this truth – that God governs the affairs of men. And if a sparrow cannot fall to the ground without His notice, is it possible an empire can rise without His aid? We have been assured, sir, in the sacred writings that, except the Lord build the house, they labor in vain that build it...I firmly believe this."

Historian C. Greg Singer points out, "Christian theism had so permeated the colonial mind that it continued to guide even those who had come to regard the gospel with indifference or even hostility."

In 1844, the United States Supreme Court studied the inception of America's spiritual roots and concluded, "Our laws and our institutions must necessarily be based on and must embody the teachings of the Redeemer of mankind." The nation's Highest Court cited 87 distinctive historical and legal precedents from the founding fathers, the congresses, and the state governments. Clearly, the very core of the United States of America's foundation is rooted in the Bible and the gospel message of Jesus Christ.

Three Factors That Always Precede a Nation's Collapse

The world has observed many great nations and empires come and go. Without prejudice, the archives of history divulge three distinct indicators present in every nation just prior to its collapse – social decay, cultural decay, and moral decay.

Social Decay

Social decay is evidenced by a loss of economic discipline that often is incited by an out-of-control, expanding bureaucracy of governmental mandates and "red tape." This compels small business owners to leave the marketplace as a result of no longer being able to run a profitable enterprise.

The Affordable Care Act, otherwise known as Obamacare, is the largest government takeover of American free enterprise the United States has ever envisaged. Thousands of small

Can America Be Spared?

businesses are projected to be driven out of the marketplace as a result of their inability to comply with the governmental mandates inherent within Obamacare. Any business or individual failing to conform to these new mandates will receive monetary fines and or penalties to be enforced by the IRS!

Representative John Fleming from Louisiana said, "Obamacare is the most dangerous piece of legislation ever passed in Congress. It is the most existential threat to our economy that the country has seen since the Great Depression."

In November 2014, Jonathan Gruber, a professor at MIT and an architect of Obamacare, admitted that the Obama administration went through "tortuous" measures to keep the facts about the legislation from the American people, saying, "Yeah, we lied to the 'stupid' American people to get it passed."

In the words of one of our nation's founding fathers, Patrick Henry, "The liberties of a people never were, nor ever will be, secure, when the transactions of their rulers may be concealed from them."

Lawlessness within society always occurs when an out-of-control government lies to its citizens. Human trafficking of our young girls as kidnapped, forced labor in the sex trade industry is a $32 billion business globally in which the United States has become the leading benefactor. And while our society is plummeting to the lowest levels of possible decay, those of us who are Christians seem content to hide behind the walls of our million dollar church buildings singing "Kumbaya" – pretending that our precious daughters are really not the latest prey of America's newest, Las Vegas business cartel.

Cultural Decay

When there is a breach and a weakening of the historical standards and norms of tradition, sensibility, and principle upon which a nation is founded and governed, cultural decay follows and the "Rule of Law" is replace by lawlessness and tyranny.

The once, highly revered United States Constitution, traditionally served as the foundation and bedrock for American politics, and our Judicial System, in a society which once willfully restrained itself from tyranny by adhering to the practice of governance through the Separation of Powers in the various branches of government. Today, however, the freedom for Americans to vote on critical issues means nothing as radical judges autonomously ignore our country's governing documents by legislating from the bench, and overturning the majority vote of hard-working, tax-paying citizens.

As cited by Brant Clifton in *The Daily Haymaker*, in May 2012, 61% of North Carolina citizens voted that marriage shall be defined as being between a man and a woman. The U.S. Supreme Court declined to hear challenges to the same-sex laws in North Carolina and other states, saying that it was an issue to be decided within the states. That, however, did not stop federal judge Max Cogburn of Asheville from sticking his nose into the affair, overturning the law, and declaring the vote by the North Carolina citizens as unconstitutional. We are slipping into a very dangerous time when unaccountable, radical judges, on the basis of personal beliefs, wipe out a law approved by the people and their elected representatives.

In Montana, nearly 80% of voters turned out and approved a state referendum requiring government officials to conduct immigration checks on anyone seeking services provided by the state. The purpose of the law is to ensure that people who are in the U.S. illegally are not hired for government jobs. District Judge Jeffrey Sherlock struck down the decision made by Montana's voters, saying, "...that it conflicts with federal immigration laws." The forfeiture of one's constitutional freedoms, like voting, always follows the loss of religious liberty!

Moral Decay

Moral decay is the final, and most telltale sign, indicating that a nation is in the concluding stages of collapse. In almost every historical case, the decline in morality goes unrecognized as the citizens perceive the weakening of moral values as new found freedom and emancipation from the constraints of lifestyle choices that were imposed upon them. Just take a look at what has happened to America in the last 50 years.

1. In 1962, the US Supreme Court removed prayer from our public schools.

2. Since the landmark *Roe v. Wade* decision of 1973, there have been 60 million abortions in the United States.

3. The reason for 95% of all abortions performed is that the woman simply did not want the baby. Rape or incest had absolutely nothing to do with the decision.

4. As of 2014, 41% of all children in America are born out of wedlock.

5. Between 2006 and 2010, nearly half of all heterosexual women (48%) age 15 to 44, said they were not married to their spouse or partner when they first cohabited with them. That's up from 43% in 2002 and 34% in 1995.

6. 61% of Christians believe that sexual relations outside of marriage are perfectly acceptable, while 56% of Christians believe "cohabitation" is appropriate.

7. A surprising 50% of Christians believe that voting for a pro-abortion candidate is perfectly acceptable if that politician supports other social issues that will advance the economy.

8. What was once considered the murder of an unborn child is now casually discussed, even amongst Christians, as *"a woman's right to choose."*

9. As of 2014, 59% of all Americans support same-sex marriage.

10. Human trafficking of young girls as kidnapped, forced labor in the sex-trade industry has become the new multi-billion dollar business in America.

America in Final Stages of Decline

Can anyone read these statistics and dispute the fact that America is in its final stages of decline and racing towards an irreparable apocalypse?

Consider these sobering words from the former U.S. Education Secretary William Bennett.

"National prosperity, as it happens, is largely dependent on lots of good private character. If lying, manipulations, sloth, lack of discipline, and personal responsibility become commonplace, the national economy grinds down. A society that produces street predators and white-collar criminals has to pay for prison cells. A society in which drug use is rampant must pay for drug treatment centers. The breaking up of families means many more foster homes and lower high school graduation rates. A society that is parsimonious in its personal charity (in terms of both time and money) will require more government welfare. Just as there are enormous financial benefits to moral health, there are enormous financial costs to moral collapse."

Is There Still Hope for America?

America seems to be aligned on the same path of ultimate destruction that was pioneered by Rome and authenticated in its tragic fall. Given the past historical record of empires, and with the assumption that America continues on its current path, the impending outcome of apocalypse is quite predictable.

Why do declining nations fail to correct their problems? Simple, a disintegrating civilization typically will not recognize the stage or severity of their decay until it is too late. And in America, even those of us in the Church have been lulled into believing that our nation is just too big and powerful to collapse.

Yet God will deliver a nation that responds to His warning. Facing imminent slaughter by the armies of Moab and Ammon, the kingdom of Judah humbled itself, sought God, and was spared a horrific collapse (2 Chronicles chapter 20).

Sent by God to warn the Assyrian kingdom, Jonah traveled to the capital city, Nineveh, along the Tigris River. Jonah walked the streets screaming with passionate conviction, "*...forty more days and Nineveh will be overthrown*" (Jonah 3:4).

Assyria was an incredible civilization whose rule over Mesopotamia dates back to 2400 BC until its fall in 612 BC. Nineveh, its capital city, was spectacular! Many scientific, philosophical, and practical advances to humanity were pioneered by the Assyrian populace. The Assyrians invented locks and keys for doors, a system for keeping time, paved roads, the first postal system, the first use of iron, libraries, plumbing, and, believe it or not, flush toilets.

The Assyrians believed Jonah's warning, repented of their evil ways, and God spared their nation. Nineveh continued to flourish for an additional 200 years until their moral values, again eroded, and the once, great empire collapsed in 612 BC.

Today, the handwriting is on the wall for America. Unless we repent individually and nationally we will continue to spiral into a moral decline of certain collapse. The warning signs are all around us as we become more and more decadent and immoral. Every great nation that has traveled this road in the annals of history's past is no longer here to tell us they wish they had listened to God and had chosen a different path.

Myles Holmes, pastor of Revive Church in Collinsville, IL, cites a vital yet often neglected distinction regarding America's wealth, prestige, and security, saying,

Can America Be Spared?

"Many conservative patriots are confused theologically and historically regarding a simple but strategic virtue – believing that God chose America, and thus, the United States has been blessed. God, however, did not choose America. America chose God. America's Founding Fathers were men of faith who chose to worship God, obey His commandments, and to establish the United States and its principles upon the eternal Word of God. Thus, America has enjoyed favor and blessing because its Founders chose to honor and obey God. America's current choice to turn away from God will result in God removing His hand of protection and blessing from the United States. The opposite of God's protection and favor is judgment. America is living on borrowed money, borrowed time, and borrowed obedience. America must wake up! The time to repent was passed a long time ago!"

There is still time for America to repent, but will we listen to God's warnings? Will we pay attention to the warnings of history and all that remains from nations that were once so sovereign and mighty – a few, leftover museum artifacts with a voice that echoes from their broken edifices, pleading with future generations, *"Turn before it's too late?"* Will we heed the few brave messengers who have been scoffed at for trying to stop us from driving our nation over a cliff? Will we listen to the warning of this book?

Chapter Six
The Church's Last Call

In preparing to write this chapter my heart is deeply grieved for America and the American church. I wish my message was wonderful, lighthearted, and full of laughter, joy, and great financial prosperity. That, however, is not what God has placed on my heart.

In 1998, David Wilkerson authored a riveting book, titled, *America's Last Call*. How ironic, for the past year Brother Wilkerson's volume has been sitting on the left side of my desk, in clear view. With a cup of coffee in hand the book's title caught my eye, and the Holy Spirit's nudge was so clear; *"Kim, this is The Church's Last Call."*

The Destruction of London

Many Christians, pastors, and churches populated the wealthy, world class city of London in 1665. In fact, London's wealth was so vast, that the city was known as the "Jewel of the British Empire." With colonies, lands, and investments worldwide, the sun literally never set on the British Empire!

The Coming American Apocalypse

Known as a Christian city, London had many great churches, preachers, and was a towering center for religious activities.

London's vast amounts of wealth began to corrupt the multitudes. Unemployment skyrocketed. People began indulging in their fleshly lusts. Atheism and agnosticism became popular. Fornication and prostitution spread throughout the city.

Several fiery preachers like Richard Baxter and John Owen were forewarned by God of London's coming destruction. These men warned of coming judgments, pestilence, the collapse of businesses, and fires that would burn throughout the city, but no one believed them. Not even the Christians. Many laughed, mocked, and said, *"How can the most prosperous city on earth suddenly fall to devastation, fire, and pestilence?"*

In 1665, a terrible plague compassed the great city. Thousands of people died. Bodies were piled on wooden carts and the poor were buried in mass graves. Pestilence visited every street exactly as prophesied! Just when the plague appeared to be ending and all seemed to be returning to normal, on September 2, 1666, a small fire started in the bakeshop of Thomas Farynor, baker to King Charles II. Spreading through London quickly, the fire burned for four days. Some 430 acres, 13,000 houses, 89 churches, and 52 Guild Halls were destroyed. Thousands of people found themselves homeless as 80% of London was completely destroyed in 96 hours!

The Puritan, John Owen, wrote, *"Ah, London, London! How long has the Lord been striving with thee by His Spirit, by His word, by His messengers..."*

The Church's Last Call

After the burning of London, the Knight Sir Edward Turner made the following statement in a speech that he gave to the king and the convening of Parliament.

> *"We must forever with humility acknowledge the justice of God in punishing this whole nation by the late dreadful conflagration of London. We know they were not the greatest sinners on whom the tower of Siloam fell and doubtless all our sins did contribute to the filling of that measure, which being full, drew down the wrath of God upon that city..."*

After Turner's speech the king responded as follows:

> *"His Majesty therefore, out of a deep and pious sense of what himself and all his people now suffer, and with a religious care to prevent what may yet be feared, unless it shall please Almighty God to turn away his anger from us, doth hereby publish and declare his Royal will and pleasure, that Wednesday, being the tenth of October next ensuing, shall be set apart, and kept, and observed by all his Majesty's subjects of England and Wales...as a day of solemn fasting and humiliation, to implore the mercies of God, that it would please him to pardon the crying sins of this nation, those especially which have drawn down this last and heavy judgment upon us, and to remove from us all other his judgments which our sins have deserved, and which we now either feel or fear... not only the blessed Scriptures, but also king and Parliament, do roundly conclude that it was for our sins, our manifold iniquities, our crying sins, that God has sent this heavy judgment upon us."*

Although London was rebuilt, the city never regained its glory!

Obedience or Disobedience

Just like the once, valiant city of London, the United States is overflowing with many great churches, preachers, and Christians. And yet, the Church in America has lost nearly all of its influence. We have become euphoric with our newly discovered ability to make our voice known in Washington by casting our vote behind the privacy of a closed curtain at the ballot box. We find solace and contentment in the fact that we, as Christians, stormed the polls in massive numbers to vote on Election Day. Then, as if we are viewing a sporting event on a large screen HDTV, we slowly watch our nation die in full digitized living color, while we hide behind the four walls of our million dollar church buildings, criticizing our wicked politicians for our nation's plight, and feeling justified because, after all, we voted.

Should we exercise our Constitutional responsibility and vote? Of course! But when Jesus returns, He is not going to ask us if we voted! Christ is going to want to know...Did you feed Me when I was hungry? Give Me a drink when I was thirsty? Take Me in when I was homeless? Clothe Me when I was naked? Care for Me when I was sick? And visit Me when I was in prison? (Matthew 25:34-46).

We have become so drunk with the wine of our own piety that we are flunking the sobriety test of life – emanating an *"I don't care attitude"* as we stagger past the most needy people in our communities. Instead of praying for our politicians and offering them our assistance, we blame them for our nation's decline, saying, *"...praise the Lord,"* in one breath, only to publicly slander them from the privacy of our Facebook and Twitter pulpits, with our next breath. And we do all of this not even caring that the homeless person we just ignored is a Wounded Warrior – a Veteran who sacrificed everything to secure the freedoms all of us enjoy.

Instead of worshipping the God of the Bible, we are now worshipping the god of politics at the voting booth! And please do not take these statements out of context or misquote the author of this book. I firmly believe that every American citizen, including Christians, have a duty to exercise their Constitutional responsibility to vote when there is an election! At the same time, however, God never said he would spare our nation if we voted. God said He would *forgive our sin and restore our nation* when we, as Christians decide to HUMBLE ourselves, PRAY and SEEK God's face, and TURN from OUR WICKED ways.

The fate of our nation does not rest upon what our government does. The fate of our nation hangs in the balance of what we, as Christians, decide to do. Will we as Americans (like the Christians who lived in London during its destruction in 1666), continue to ignore all the warning signs of moral decay and the impending collapse of our nation, and continue to point our fingers at one another, and at our politicians, while we do nothing to serve and assist our communities? Or, will we humble ourselves, pray, seek the face of God, and turn from our wicked ways of neglecting the poor and needy people who live around us?

The hope and future of America will be determined by the obedience or disobedience of God's people. Moses said, "*I have set before you life and death, blessing and cursing; therefore choose life, that both you and your descendants may live"* *(Deuteronomy 30:19).* The choice is ours. This is "The Church's Last Call!"

Chapter Seven
Restoring Our Influence

For those who may think that I am some kind of doomsday preacher, that is not the case. We have the greatest opportunity that any generation in America has ever been afforded, and yet, we are miserably failing to capitalize on the Triple Crown acclaimed, Secretariat *"gift horse"* that has been delivered to our doorstep, free of charge!

As ministers, we have become so busy competing against one another to see, who among us, will boast the largest congregations, build the most elaborate facilities, write the most best-selling books, drive the hottest cars, fly the fastest jets, or be seen of men on the most television stations; that we have forgotten how to humble ourselves and serve. Leading people to Jesus has never been so easy. Today's generation, however, will not listen to our *"sermons,"* they listen to our *"serving."* We have the capacity to completely turn our communities upside down and transform our nation. But we cannot do this without *"influence,"* and today's church has all but lost all of its *"influence."*

Can we, as the Church, regain the influence that we have lost? Yes! But we must understand that *"influence"* is a fruit that grows in the soil of laying down our lives to serve other people.

A Farmer's Wisdom

Soon after graduating from Oral Roberts University I found myself working full-time with a landscaping crew. Except for Joe, a very hard-working man who lost his farm due to governmental regulations, all the other workers were red-necked, tobacco chewing, beer drinking good old boys. I was not able to lead, even one, of these men to Jesus.

One day, I overheard a young Hispanic man telling the rest of the crew that he had just surrendered his life to Christ and would no longer be stopping for a beer with the guys after work. Being completely astonished, I continued to listen.

This young man's girlfriend, whom he had been living with, had recently given birth to their son. He was a beautiful baby boy! With no health insurance and a job that only paid minimum wage for a salary, the medical bills alone from childbirth left them, both, with nothing. Being one month behind in their rental home payments and with the utility company threatening to turn off the power, this young father did not know what he was going to do. That weekend, however, the farmer unexpectedly showed up at the small home they were renting just outside of town. After cutting their grass and helping to clean the home this young couple rented, Joe blessed them with diapers for their son, groceries that he had purchased at the store, $50 cash, and he also paid their past due rent and utility bills.

Restoring Our Influence

As the crew continued to listen, I heard this young Hispanic man say, "Joe is a real Christian. He is not some fake, phony hypocrite. He didn't throw some track in my face or put me down for not being married to my girlfriend. He cut my grass and paid my bills. I did not even tell him that I had a need. He just noticed. Then, he showed up early Sunday morning to take me, my girlfriend, and my son to church. I was reluctant to go, but I couldn't say no, because I knew this guy was for real. When the offering plate was coming by Joe tapped me on the shoulder and told me not to worry about giving anything because he had taken care of putting something in the plate for me. After that, I don't know what happened. The pastor preached a sermon, something happened in my heart, and I knew I needed to give my life to Christ. So I raised my hand, walked to the altar, gave my life to Jesus, and I feel like a new person. On top of this, my girlfriend and I are getting married next week. Joe is going to be my best man and the pastor at that church is going to perform the wedding."

This old country farmer knew that taking an interest in other people, and going out of one's way to care for, serve, and meet the needs of those in our communities, opens the hearts of dads, moms, business owners, politicians, and teenagers – and gives us influence. A hurting, single mom may harden her heart and curse a *"sarcastic saint,"* but she will lower her protective walls and listen to a *"selfless servant"* who purchases diapers and formula for her baby. Jesus said, *"I have come to serve" (Luke 22:27).* What in the world are we doing?

Pride, a Dangerous Enemy

After two thousand years there really has not been much change in human behavior. Today's preachers struggle with the same issues faced by every generation: Power, sex, and money!

Just minutes after freshly consecrating their lives to God while partaking in The Last Supper with Christ, the disciples began to argue over which one of them would be the greatest. Responding with a blunt reality check regarding those in history who would be known for possessing the most ostentatious and paramount of ministries, Jesus did not even casually mention apostles, prophets, evangelists, pastors, or teachers – instead, He handed the trophy for living the most significant life to those who serve. I cannot help but wonder if Mother Teresa is first on that list.

24 Within minutes they were bickering over who of them would end up the greatest.
25 But Jesus intervened: "Kings like to throw their weight around and people in authority like to give themselves fancy titles.
26 It's not going to be that way with you. Let the senior among you become like the junior; let the leader act the part of the servant.
27 Who would you rather be: The one who eats the dinner or the one who serves the dinner? You'd rather eat and be served, right? But I have taken my place among you as the one who serves."

Luke 22:24-27 MSG

Okay. If Jesus, the One who holds All Authority, All Might, All Power, All Majesty, and All Dominion, stated in simple, clear, easy to understand language, that He took His place among us as One who serves; then I have a question: What in the world are we American preachers doing?

In the preceding 30 years I have observed more movements than I care to discuss. I have witnessed The Latter Rain Movement, The Word Movement, The Faith Movement, The Prosperity Movement, The Prophetic Movement, and the Apostolic Movement. As ministers of Christ, we have seized claim to more titles than all of the epithets archived in the annals of The Library of Congress, combined! Could we possibly have a Humble Servant Movement, or maybe even, a Feeding the Poor Movement?

No human ever outgrows the need to humble one's self before Christ. The pride within our own flesh is far more deceptive than the egotism of this world. Anything short of a thorough work of Christ's applied grace in our hearts leaves us vulnerable to the unrestrained, deep-seated conceit in our own flesh. Conquering Satan is easy. Mastering our own selfish pride, for some, requires a lifetime just to comprehend that "we" are the real problem.

For those of us in ministry, unrestrained pride arouses our emotions. We start perceiving ourselves to be more important than we actually are. Instead of seeking to serve other people, we pursue degrees, titles, fame, and accolades. Instead of feeding the poor we feed our inflated egos and abnegate Christ's command to win the lost in order to gain the praises of men. In lieu of building disciples we construct elaborate buildings and monuments. Make no mistake about it, the pride within our own flesh is cunning, deceptive, and has seduced many to believe that *"serving"* is not necessary. Pride is a treacherous enemy!

Jesus Is Serious About Serving

Pride has an ingenious side to its demise that will inspire us to justify *"burying our talents"* and our disregard for the neediest people in our communities. As one pastor told me, "...our target groups are wealthy business owners...feeding the poor is not part of our vision." Wait a minute. Each local church has a unique, distinctive vision. All of us, however, have precisely the same mission – which is to preach the gospel message of Jesus Christ and to care for the impoverished and indigent people in our communities.

When Christ returns, He will not have one list of questions for pastors and another list of questions for parishioners. Jesus is going to ask His apostles, prophets, evangelists, pastors, and teachers precisely the same questions that He requires from everyone, *"Did you FEED Me when I was hungry? Give Me a DRINK when I was thirsty? TAKE ME IN when I was homeless? CLOTHE Me when I was naked? CARE for Me when I was sick? VISIT Me when I was in prison?"* (Matthew 25:34-46). For those who disobey, Christ will say, *"...Get out...you're good for nothing but the fires of hell"* (Matthew 25:41 MSG).

The Hard Facts

According to a *Charisma* magazine article, only 3% of all contributions donated to the average church are actually expended to assist or minister to non-Christians. A study conducted by The Evangelical Credit Union concluded that the typical church in America only allocates 1% of its budget towards aiding the poor, while an astounding 82% to 86% of all incoming resources are consumed on buildings, personnel, and administrative expenses.

Could our own behavior actually be part of the reasons why the Church has lost its influence and people would rather not listen to us? Maybe we had better ask ourselves the hard questions, like, are the current practices of the average American church (like spending 96% of our budgets on ourselves), combined with our failure to obey Christ and care for the poor and needy, part of the reasons why several members of the United States Senate are calling for the Church's tax-exempt status to be revoked?

Please don't write letters and send emails to inform this book's author of the numerous churches that reach out to the poor and sacrificially serve the needs and the needy people in their communities. Yes, there are some churches doing this, but not many, and certainly not a majority.

If we are serious about obeying Christ and willing to take a good look at ourselves in the mirror, we would discover that most churches, including Pentecostals and Evangelicals, do next to nothing when it comes to practically serving the needs of those who are among the least fortunate amongst us. So, if we neglect to conduct a serious examination of how we manage our ministries, and fail to ask ourselves the tough questions; Big Brother is going to come in and put a microscope over all of our churches and demand that we pay our fair share. Sadly, we will have no one to blame but ourselves!

A Matter of Simple Choice

Located in California's Simi Valley, *Charisma* magazine also cited Cornerstone Church's commitment to give away 55% of all incoming ministry revenue. According to *Charisma*, Pastor Francis Chan often asks, "Do our actions show that we really believe that our money belongs to God?" Staff members at Cornerstone have tried to model financial generosity in a number of ways. Some have raided their retirement accounts and given money to organizations serving the poor and needy in their community. This example, from *"Leaders Who Lead,"* has inspired a lifestyle of generosity to spread to other church members. Some have chosen to downsize into smaller, modest homes in order to have additional funds available to assist the poor. This really boils down to a matter of simple choice. Do we wish to be Self-centered or Christ-centered?

Confronted with the reality that their current facility was hindering growth, the Cornerstone leadership faced a difficult choice. Pastor Chan and the pastoral staff brought in consultants and architects who laid out an elaborate new campus with an extended complex of buildings, brick streets, fountains, and gardens. "I really felt it was repulsive," Chan says. "It showed us spending money for our own comfort."

Chan informed the congregation that the elaborate architectural proposal was off the table. Instead, they chose a modest design that would save millions of dollars and allow Cornerstone to continue giving away 55% of all incoming resources. Cornerstone's website conveys their united conviction regarding the Church's mission.

The Mission of Cornerstone Church
"In order to display the Gospel well, we must see missions as more than just another program of the church that competes for people and resources. We must see it as more than just what happens 'over there,' across oceans or borders or languages, as opposed to the 'church ministry' that we do here. The New Testament church did not have a 'missions program.' The Church was the missions program. Every believer is called to display Christ where God has providentially placed them. We must send people into homes, neighborhoods, workplaces, schools, social circles, and to the ends of the earth in order to join God in His mission to unite everything in Christ" (Acts 1:8).

Cornerstone's local outreach and service to their community includes strategic partnerships in various domains, including schools, public health and safety, parks and recreation, the homeless and needy, youth and family, foster care, and more. Their hope is to build genuine friendships within their city and lead people to Christ. The needs of California's Simi Valley are being served with practical, hands-on ministry and Cornerstone continues to win the hearts of people, gain influence, and grow.

If We Treasure the Right Things
A packed, exciting church meeting with all the *"bells and whistles"* that fails to change the hearts of pastors, parishioners and redirect church spending to elevate the poor and needy so they feel welcomed among us, and stir us to wash the feet of those who live in our communities, is not revival – but is only cunning, deceptive emotion. Our *"sermons"* don't influence people – it's our *"serving!"*

Jesus was so clear. *"For where your treasure is, there your heart will be also" (Matthew 6:21).* Christ was not limiting this guideline to individual spending. This principle also applies to how we, as pastors and leaders, elect to spend church revenue.

A detailed examination uncovering the percentages of how every church expends its resources will quickly reveal our purpose, direction, and focus. Are we a Self-centered church or a Christ-centered church? Are we catering to our fleshly desires or are we fulfilling God's will? Our actual spending reports will reveal the condition of our hearts as pastors and leaders. Remember, if we treasure the wrong things we will dream the wrong dreams and end up building castles in the sand. But if we treasure the right things (Jesus), we will dream the right dreams, fulfill God's will for our lives and ministries, and transform our communities and our nation.

Are We Willing To Change?

Francis Chan, pastor of Cornerstone Church, says churches are often theologically accurate when they teach about giving. But they haven't reoriented themselves. In other words, our practice does not model our preaching. We need to be willing to take a long, hard look at our church budgets, get rid of the fat, sacrifice, and focus more of our spending towards direct, practical ministry in our communities.

Reaching our society and leading people to Jesus Christ is actually very easy. In fact, the opportunities have never been so limitless. Our major cities, suburbs, towns, and rural areas are falling apart. Because the needs are very great, this means our opportunities have never been more advantageous for us to humble ourselves and serve the needs and the neediest people in our communities. Humility and serving produces the fruit of influence! As we take the time to care for other people, and serve them, their hearts will open and they will listen to us. Hurting people do not hear our SERMONS, they hear our SERVING!

If our goals are to obey Jesus, fulfill the great commission, adjust the course of our nation and prevent an impending apocalypse, then we all must be willing to humble ourselves and examine the way we implement church ministry. Currently, pastors, leaders, and Christians, as a whole, have very little influence in America. This, however, is easy to change. Are we willing to roll up our sleeves and SERVE instead of SIT? The entire philosophy of church in America has digressed to a COME, SIT, LISTEN, and GO mentality. We COME to church, SIT, LISTEN to a well-prepared message or elaborately choreographed entertainment, and then we GO live our lives as we please – not even noticing that the young girl in the checkout line at the grocery store is a struggling, single mom trying to figure out how to care for her baby. These are the COME, SIT, LISTEN, and GO people. They are everywhere! This type of conduct is perceived as being hypocritical to all who observe our conduct and is disgusting to Jesus.

Christ's idea of church is simple; as pastors and parishioners, we assemble together, worship, and allow God to change us into a team of selfless servants that expend our time, talents, and resources to help elevate the status of the neediest people in our communities and lead them to Jesus.

Who Is Responsible?
Let's stop blaming the government for our nation's moral decline and aim our pointed fingers at ourselves. Our government is not capable of altering or adjusting the direction of America. Only we, as the Church, are capable of doing this.

Can we transform the course of our nation? Absolutely! But we must humbly acknowledge that the self-centered way that we have been conducting ministry is responsible for turning people off to the gospel message, and has caused us to lose our influence. Can we recapture the influence that the American Church once possessed? Yes! But, all of us will need to cooperate by participating in the following prerogatives or we are going to lose this great nation.

1. Humble Ourselves
As apostles, prophets, evangelists, pastors, teachers, and leaders, we must humble ourselves and model the type of attitudes and behaviors that God requires out of us as *"Leaders Who Lead."* Humility denotes accepting the responsibilities that accompany leadership and requires that we hold ourselves accountable to do something about our nation's moral decay. Instead of pointing fingers and blaming our politicians, we must own up to the fact that we, too, have caused some of the problems our nation is facing. We must face the truth and be willing to initiate concrete changes in how we shepherd our ministries. Anything less is not true humility.

2. Pray and Seek God's Face
We must pray until we know, that we know, that we know...that we genuinely have had an encounter with God Himself.

One day I was walking through O'Hare Airport in Chicago and saw a young man from a different religious persuasion praying alone in a corner. I tapped the young man on the shoulder and asked who he was talking to. His exact response was, "I'm not talking to anyone I am just saying prayers." While walking away the Lord nudged my heart and quietly said, *"That's what's wrong with too many of My people. Instead of talking with Me they are just saying prayers."*

Consistency in prayer is very difficult when there is no genuine relationship with God, and we are *"just saying prayers."* As pastors and parishioners, we must have a fresh, life-changing encounter with Christ. Our relationship with God must be current and real.

3. Turn from Our Wicked Ways
Can we all be real with ourselves for a moment? Would God actually tell us, as pastors and leaders, to turn from our wicked ways if there were not any things that we needed to turn away from? Let's take the time to find out what God hates about our ministries and make some necessary changes.

4. God Will Forgive Our Sin
If we confess our sins, God is faithful to forgive us (1 John 1:9). Let's be mindful to extend this same forgiveness to those who have sinned against us, including our political leaders.

5. God Will Heal Our Land
Healing for our nation will come as God's response to the choices that we, as pastors and leaders in the Body of Christ, make. When we as apostles, prophets, evangelists, pastors, and teachers humble ourselves, pray and seek the face of God, and

adjust the things God hates about our ministries – then God will hear from heaven, forgive our sin, and heal our nation.

"Influence" is a fruit that grows in the soil of laying down our lives to serve other people. Our nation is on the verge of collapse. The time has come for all of us in every denomination, to lay aside our preferences and prejudices, to band together as a team, merge our resources, and serve the needs, and the neediest people, in our communities. Today's generation do not hear our *"sermons,"* they hear our *"serving."* Serving the needs of others is something that all of us, in every denomination, can agree on. Let's humble ourselves, join together as one united army of *"Leaders Who Lead,"* by serving, and take our nation back!

Influence is a fruit that grows in the soil of laying down our lives to serve other people!

Chapter Eight
Ferguson, a Wake-Up Call

On August 9, 2014, 18-year-old Michael Brown, a black teenager, was fatally shot by Darren Wilson, a 28-year-old white police officer in the St. Louis suburb of Ferguson, Missouri. The shooting ignited protests and unrest in Ferguson, partially due to the belief, held by some, that Brown was surrendering, as well as long-standing racial tensions between the majority-black Ferguson community and the majority-white city government and police force.

After nearly 3 months of investigating all the eyewitness testimonies and forensic evidence, a St. Louis County grand jury declined to indict Police Officer Darren Wilson. The decision by the grand jury sparked, both, peaceful and violent protests in Chicago, Salt Lake City, Washington DC, Philadelphia, New York, Oakland, and other major cities across America.

On the eve of the grand jury's verdict, however, Ferguson literally was set on fire. Without anywhere near enough manpower to stop the angry protesters, the only thing Ferguson police officers, the fire department, and the National Guard could do, was watch in horror as more than 20 businesses burnt to the ground while others were ransacked, looted, and destroyed.

Ferguson is a Warning
The protests, riots, violence, and fires in Ferguson, Missouri are just the initial birth pangs of America's eminent collapse. As a nation we have turned our back on God, common sense, and morality. If we fail to act now, the perils of Ferguson, in conjunction with rising unemployment, a heightened threat of terrorism, and an out-of-control Federal government will spread to every major city in America and ignite our anger and deep-seated bitterness into an inferno of a fulminating apocalypse.

America and the American Church are asleep. We have sat on the sidelines as bystanders, doing nothing, for too long. Content to remain hidden behind the four walls of our church buildings, we have been pretending that our nation's problems will disappear if we just pray hard enough. And then we have the audacity to call this, faith, and say things like "...well, we just have to trust God." As Kenneth E. Hagin used to say, "...that is just ignorance gone to seed."

Real faith is to obey God which results in the fruit of "Genuine Revival." Myles Holmes, pastor of Revive Church in Collinsville, IL says,

> *"Much of the church has it completely backwards. In their desperate demand for an 'experience,' many ignore the fact that God is much more concerned with our obedience. Thus, there is constant confusion and*

deception. If we will concentrate on obeying, we will never lack the miraculous!"

Seeds of Racism

Racism is not just a problem in the south. Systematic racism has been an unrecognized blight on the northern states during America's entire history. For those of us who are Caucasian, this is very difficult to understand because we have not faced the experience of being under constant suspicion from the authorities, or being denied opportunities due to our skin color.

In addition to the normal battles of life that all of us face, even today, many African-Americans still find themselves combating the grim reality of lingering racism that is reemerging in our society as seeds sprouting up from the soil of our nation's history. Although no one condones violence and the egregious criminal acts of vandalism, fire-setting, and looting as solutions, the time has come for every American to acknowledge that our country is facing momentous issues that will take all of us down a road to collapse if we fail to respond now.

Dr. Alveda King, the niece of famed civil rights leader Martin Luther King, Jr., condemned the Ferguson riots, looting, and fire-setting as an *"unnecessary evil"* that has done nothing other than to set back race relations in America.

As pastors, leaders, and Christians, we cannot continue to put a Band-Aid over America's real, deep-seated nuisances with another series of self-help messages. We must stop deceiving ourselves into thinking that everything will just be okay. In order for our nation to be healed, we must humble ourselves and acknowledge the acts of hatred and prejudicial sins committed by our forefathers and own up to any underlying attitudes and prejudices that may be lingering in our own hearts.

We Must Act Now

Unlike many, I believe there is hope for America. God still has a plan and purpose for our nation. We don't have to allow our country to go to hell in a hand basket. We have unlimited opportunities and a bright future. But we must respond now!

Trying to assemble church congregations from various denominations to pray and worship together is practically impossible. So let's not focus on trying to be ecumenical and hold joint services. Instead, let's unite our faith, dynamisms, and finances and do something with which we all can unanimously agree – *serve the needs and the neediest people in our communities!*

We Can Change Our Nation by Serving

Serving the practical needs of people has a miraculous way of bringing healing to a population. If, instead of debating with each other over inconsequential differences, we choose to band together as a cross-denominational team of volunteers, we will serve our community's needs and bring healing to our nation.

This will take courage, organization, and cooperation. First, let's be proactive in taking advantage of the wisdom and benefits that come to those who examine their budgets and actual spending reports. Statistics reveal that the average American church, including Evangelicals and Pentecostals, only spends a grand total of 1% of all incoming resources to aid the poor and needy in our communities, while 96% is directed internally. Jesus revealed that we locate the focus and intent of our hearts by

Ferguson, a Wake-up Call

conducting a non-biased audit of how we spend God's money. For when we treasure the right things (Jesus), we will dream the right dreams and our visions and church ministries will be pure.

In 2 Chronicles 7:14, God implores, us as leaders, to pray and seek His face, and to ask ourselves *"the hard questions,"* so the Holy Spirit may search our hearts and show us where we need to make changes in how we execute ministry. Are we Self-centered or Christ-centered? As apostles, prophets, evangelists, pastors, and teachers, let's courageously ask God where and how we may need to adjust financial spending in our churches and ministries. There are many needs, which mean there are many opportunities that we may capitalize on, if we choose to do so.

If we courageously face ourselves, and our flaws, we can humbly adjust how we conduct ministry and become part of the solution to our nation's ills. Government cannot do this, but we as the Church can do this if we will band together and obey Christ. If we sacrifice NOW, and SERVE our communities TODAY – America will be healed TOMORROW.

We don't have to live in a nation filled with violence, corruption, moral decay, and thousands of fires burning our major American cities to mere ashes.

The wakeup call and warning of Ferguson, Missouri need not become the next reality TV show highlighting the collapse of every, major American city. For if we as pastors and parishioners, business owners and leaders, would humble ourselves, pray and seek God's face, turn from our wicked ways, examine and restructure our church budgets and passionately serve our communities' needs, joining together as a cross-denominational infantry of selfless servants – we can revolutionize America's future by SERVING.

Chapter Nine
Dining With Zacchaeus

The abilities we possess to impact our communities are limitless if we would just use our influence. Our civic leaders, along with local and national politicians, have no answers for the problems that plague American society. With rising crime, an overloaded prison system, outdated power grids, roads and interstates in disrepair, and 70,000 bridges needing immediate replacement at a cost of $72 billion; government has no clue where the money is going to come from to repair and maintain our nation's aged infrastructure.

Love Your Nation by Serving

Egypt was one of the world's greatest dynasties. After consulting with the chief administrator and all of his advisers, the Pharaoh had no idea how to navigate through the escalating problems facing his nation. After a restless night with no sleep and a reoccurring dream that would not leave his mind, the Egyptian king summoned Joseph, a young Jewish prisoner, to appear before his throne.

Joseph was different than all of the other prisoners. Not only was he known for his keen ability to discern God's will, but as an outsider and a foreigner, Joseph loved Egypt as if it was his own country. He demonstrated loyalty to the nation by serving in the prison where he was confined to captivity.

When was the last time that we as apostles, prophets, evangelists, pastors, teachers, and leaders, have visited our State's Senators, our Mayor, or other Community or Civic Leaders; to inquire how we may volunteer, help, and serve? Let's just be real for a moment. Have we ever done this? And if the answer is no, then why should they listen to us?

Live Your Faith in the Public Arena

As a genuine *"Leader Who Leads,"* making himself available to serve a godless king is something Joseph, and every Jew, considered a normal part of living a godly, holy life. Why? This is because our commitment to Christ is demonstrated by serving other people, including key individuals, along with civic and political leaders (1 Peter 2:17).

An important, but often neglected part of influencing elected, public officials occurs when we *"live our faith,"* without compromising our values, right in front of their eyes. This, however, can only occur when we include *"rubbing shoulders"* with our elected representatives, as a normal part of our protocol as pastors and leaders.

Because Joseph made himself available to volunteer and serve his Egyptian community, the Pharaoh felt comfortable sharing his deepest concerns and requested advice regarding a dream. Joseph politely and purposefully, lived his faith right in front of the king, saying, *"...God will give Pharaoh the answer he desires" (Genesis 41:16 NIV).*

Dining with Zacchaeus

Joseph's reply was the equivalent of you, as a pastor or leader, visiting the mayor of your city, making yourself available to serve, listening to his heart, and validating your relationship with Christ by saying, "let's have a word of prayer, together, and God will provide the wisdom you need." Then, with the type of honor and confidence only a true servant understands; you extend your arm, take his hand, and demonstrate what being a *"Leader Who Leads"* is by praying with your mayor.

Far, too, often we timidly say, "I'll keep you in prayer" or, "I'll be praying for you." And we say this while we're standing right there with someone who needs Christ. Why not pray for the individual while we are with them? As John Stossel would say, "Give me a break!" That's compromise! Are we ashamed of Jesus? Are we fearful or embarrassed to live our faith in front of other people, publicly?

Jesus said that if we acknowledge Him in front of other people that He will acknowledge us to the Father. If, however, we deny Christ by making the choice to not live our faith, publicly, in front of others, we will then be the ones that Christ will deny in front of the Father (Matthew 10:32-33).

How to Influence Politicians
People, including those who serve in political positions, need to observe Christ and experience His presence. How will this occur if we never rub shoulders with our Civic, Community, State, and National Leaders? They are not going to come to us; we have to go to them!

Sometimes the only thing needed to change a politician's heart is for a pastor or Christian leader to drop by and offer to help with a community project, and to live one's Christianity right in front of that elected official's eyes by taking their hand and praying with them.

We don't have to agree with a politician's views, support his policies, volunteer as a member of his reelection campaign, or even vote for him. But as pastors and leaders we can and must visit all of our elected officials, and we ought to do this often. Educating ourselves, preparing, and being up-to-date on the major issues facing our communities is vital.

During our visits, we should express appreciation for something that leader is doing, or has accomplished, to facilitate a positive difference in our community, state, or nation. Express genuine concern for his personal life. Ask how his family is doing. Are his children performing well in school and is everyone healthy? Let him know you're always available, if needed. Provide a direct, cell phone number where you may be reached in an emergency.

If a civic official is not a Christian, be a *"Leader Who Leads"* and begin to guard, care for, and shepherd his life and family. He may not know what is taking place, but that is not necessary. You are watching over his soul and providing an avenue for God to change his heart for the sake of righteousness, morality, and the common good of our nation.

In a polite, honorable demeanor, we should share our views and offer *"let's meet in the middle"* alternatives when applicable. If you are a pastor, always make yourself and your congregation available to serve or assist with vital community projects or needs. Remember, just like everyone else, politicians do not hear our *"sermons,"* they hear our *"serving."* If we want our politicians to *"listen,"* and to *"hear"* us, we must be available for them and willing to *"serve."*

The Supreme Court decision of *Roe v. Wade*, most likely, will never be overturned. In light of this, we cannot be afraid to *"reinvent"* ourselves. By cleverly redefining our position as *"pro-choice,"* we can lobby for legislation that will mandate physicians and clinics to present women in crisis with all the available choices of *"life and adoption alternatives."* In addition, we can help members of our School Boards *"buy into"* the wisdom of including *"life choices,"* in Junior High and High School curriculums – as better alternatives to abortion. Let's adjust our priorities to the wise use of our influence in order to save as many babies as possible.

Just prior to the end of an appointment with a Civic Leader, Community Official, Police or Fire Chief, School Board Member, Business Leader, Congressman or Senator – always pray for them and with them. Pray for their personal needs and for God to give them wisdom as a Community, State or National Leader. This is so important! Jesus said where two or more are gathered together in His Name, that He will be there *"in the midst of them" (Matthew 18:20).* You never know what may take place inside the inner chambers of a politician's heart when you take that official's hand and lead them into the tangible presence of Jesus by praying with them.

We Must Go and Pray With Them
After praying with the Pharaoh, Joseph outlined a detailed, administrative plan that, if implemented, would spare Egypt from a terrible famine of apocalyptic proportions. The Egyptian

king placed Joseph in charge of the entire nation and surrendered his life to the One, true Hebrew God, saying, *"...can we find anyone like this man, one in whom the Spirit of God is?"* (Genesis 41:38 NIV)

As the supreme ruler over Egypt, from the time he was a child, the Pharaoh was told that he was a god. Pharaoh did not listen to Joseph's *"sermons,"* he listened to his *"serving."* By publicly living his faith in front of Pharaoh, Joseph offered to help, and prayed with the Egyptian king. God obviously did something in Pharaoh's heart. Having a king who genuinely believed he was a god, change his mind, do a complete 180 degree turn in the opposite direction, and acknowledge the Hebrew God as the One and only true God – well, let's just say that for something like this to occur, influence is definitely needed!

Joseph lived his faith, publicly, in front of Pharaoh. He volunteered to serve his community and led the Egyptian king into God's presence by praying with him. God changed Pharaoh's heart, and the mighty Egyptian Empire was spared. The historical details of Joseph's philosophy are a picture of how we as pastors and leaders can influence our political officials and foster transformation in America.

This is a prime example of why we, as pastors and leaders, need to regularly visit our civic and community leaders, state, and national politicians – and personally pray with them.

Jesus and Zacchaeus
As a wicked tax collector for Caesar and the Roman Empire, Zacchaeus extorted money from the poorest of the poor. Hearing that Jesus was passing by, and being very small in

Dining with Zacchaeus

stature, Zacchaeus climbed a sycamore tree to acquire a view of Christ. Spotting Zacchaeus in the tree, Jesus said, *"...come down immediately, I must stay at your house today" (Luke 19:5 NIV)*.

Jesus knew that we, personally, must spend time with people in order to influence them. Because He elected to have dinner with Zacchaeus, Christ was mocked, scorned, and accused of compromising His faith. One moment in the presence of Jesus, however, altered the life of Zacchaeus forever. *"...Zacchaeus stood up and said to the Lord, 'Look, Lord! Here and now I give half of my possessions to the poor, and if I have cheated anybody out of anything, I will pay back four times the amount'" (Luke 19:8 NIV)*. Jesus commented, *"...today salvation has come to this house" (Luke 19:9 NIV)*.

We don't have to remain on the sidelines with those who merely, pray and do nothing, as our nation continues to spiral down the highway of heightened moral decay. There is no need to senselessly persist down our blind paths of thinking, "I'll wake up tomorrow and everything will be better;" while we ignorantly await the sudden arrival of thousands of apocalyptic fires prepared to reduce every, major American city to piles of ashes ready to be blown away by the next breath of wind.

All of this is unnecessary. If we as pastors and leaders will humble ourselves and surface from hiding behind our walled sanctuaries and sanctimonious ideologies, and start to *"rub shoulders"* with our Community, Civic, State, and National political officials – we can influence, both, people and our politicians, and adjust the course of our nation. Let's use our *"influence."* The time has come for all of us as pastors and leaders to humble ourselves, become *"Leaders Who Lead,"* and begin to dine with Zacchaeus.

Chapter Ten
Freedom Is Never Free

Thousands of brave men and women sacrificed, shed their blood, and paid a great price in order to draft the United States Constitution and courageously establish a foundation for liberty and the freedoms that all of us, in America, enjoy today.

After many years of brave leadership, Thomas Jefferson arrived at the following conclusion, "All tyranny needs to gain a foothold, is for people of good conscience to remain silent." And in the words of Ronald Reagan, while articulating his thoughts concerning America's future, our 40th President said, "If we lose freedom here, there is no place to escape to. This is the last stand on Earth."

Swedish Pastor Accused of Hate Crime
A 68-year-old Swedish pastor who preached a sermon on biblical prohibitions against homosexual behavior is waiting to see if the Supreme Court of Sweden will sentence him to six months in jail for violating a *"hate speech"* law.

Pastor Ake Green carefully cited Bible passages demonstrating that, sodomy, in the eyes of God, is a sin. In his message, Green also warned that because of its embracing of homosexuality, Sweden as a nation may be in acute danger of God's judgment.

At no point does Pastor Green advocate discrimination, rejection, hatred, violence, or any type of action against homosexuals other than prayer and the preaching of the gospel message of Christ. Nevertheless, he is still facing the likelihood of real, jail time due to the law enacted by the Swedish parliament in 2002 that criminalized expressions of *"disrespect"* against homosexuals. Just prior to the enactment of the law, the Swedish Prime Minister made it clear that referring to homosexual behavior as *"unnatural"* would be a criminal act.

Man Arrested For Reading Bible

In April 2011, a California highway patrolman arrested Mark Mackey and two other men for reading a Bible out loud in the parking lot of the Hemet, California DMV. At no point were these men rude, obnoxious, nor were they hindering or obstructing customers from doing business at the DMV. They were simply reading the Bible.

In fact, even though the Hemet, California, DMV was closed at the time of their arrest, Mr. Mackey and the two other men were cited with "impeding an open business." According to their attorneys' press release, "The men believed that they had a First Amendment right to free speech as they were standing in a planter within the parking lot and were located on public property. Further, they were not interfering with any business of the DMV and were not yelling or disturbing the peace."

Perform Wedding or Go To Jail
In October 2014, as reported by the Washington Times, Coeur d'Alene, Idaho, city officials have laid down the law to Christian pastors within their community, telling them bluntly via an ordinance that if they refuse to marry homosexuals, they will face jail time and fines.

Donald and Eveyln Knapp, who are both ordained pastors and residents of Coeur d'Alene, were asked by a gay couple to perform their wedding ceremony and the Knapps politely declined. Charged with a discriminatory hate crime, the Knapps now face a 180-day jail term and a $1,000 fine for each day they decline to perform the same-sex wedding.

Tolerance Is For Whom?
What in the world is happening in America? Islamic mosques and centers are allowed to freely preach and proselytize messages that undermine America – including the proclamation of Sharia law, female genital mutilation, and death to homosexuals – and this is completely accepted and tolerated if you happen to be a Muslim, hate Israel, and are strategically infiltrating our government in order to crown America as Islam's newest *caliphate.*

But when a pastor or Christian simply says they do not believe same-sex marriage is appropriate, or places homosexuality in the category of being *"sinful,"* along with adultery or fornication; *"independent thinking"* or holding a differing viewpoint, suddenly becomes a *"hate crime"* subject to criminal prosecution with possible fines and imprisonment.

Purposeful Religious Persecution

The time has come for every American to wake up and realize that the free-speech rights and religious liberties of Christians have become the prime target of radical activist groups, left-wing extremist judges, and our federal government who wish to silence those who champion conservative, moral values.

This is exactly what I foresaw on March 6, 1993, when, in an open vision, I observed a country church-type building sitting on a negotiation table in the Oval Office of the U.S. Presidency. With extreme urgency I heard the Lord's voice deep in my spirit, warning,

> *"You must understand the mystery and the meaning of the church building sitting on the negotiation table in the Oval Office of the U.S. Presidency. The day will come when legislation will pour out of Washington in Satan's attempt to cripple and stop the American Church."*

Privileges, Not Rights

Alternative lifestyle choices are privileges, not rights! One individual's freedom cannot suddenly become a criminal act on the part of another person who may oppose, disagree with, or hold a different opinion regarding the liberty, or choice, of another human being.

We are either all free to make choices, think independently, hold differing viewpoints, and freely speak our minds on any issues, subjects, topics, current events, or beliefs – or, we are all in the process of being stripped naked of our God-given clothing of life, liberty, and the pursuit of happiness by an out-of-control government that disregards its own Constitution in order to rape, sodomize, and violate the free-speech rights and religious liberties inherently owned from the moment of conception, by every American citizen.

The Bible is the New *"Hate Speech"*

The author of this book does not support discrimination, rejection, persecution, hatred, or violence against any human being, regardless of how someone chooses to live their life.

If a husband or wife chooses to commit *"adultery"* and have sexual relations with another individual outside of their marriage covenant, according to the Bible, a sin is being committed that will initiate a lot of hurt, pain, and anger in that person's entire family.

Likewise, if a young man and woman prefer to have sex or live together without the commitment of marriage, they, too, are committing the sin of *"fornication"* which will result in the heartache of possibly contracting numerous STD's and produce emotional instability in children due to the lack of security which comes from not having a stable home patterned after the Biblical model.

In the same manner, Scripture also cites *"homosexuality"* as the sin of rejecting and replacing God's established order for sexuality, marriage, and the family (Romans 1:25), with alternative lifestyle structures, that, like adultery and fornication, are known to cause anger, hurt, and separation within families, and foster gender identity confusion and emotional instability in children.

The Christian message has always been simple; no one is to be condemned by another human *"...for all have sinned and fall short of the glory of God" (Romans 3:23)*. Salvation and forgiveness of all sin is available through Jesus Christ (1 John 1:9). And, even if we believe something is perfectly acceptable to do in spite of the fact that Scripture lists that behavior as a sin; then we are encouraged to not do it because there is a high risk that someone else may be hurt by choosing to ignore the Bible (1 Corinthians 8:10-13).

Christians Are the New Criminals

So, are pastors and Christians suddenly guilty of *"hate speech"* and *"hate crimes,"* for publicly agreeing with a book that has been in print for more than 2,000 years? Are ministers who establish their lives and families upon the long-standing Judeo-Christian principles of the Bible, suddenly, guilty of discrimination and *"hate crimes"* for respectfully declining to perform same-sex weddings, because to do so, would violate their faith, conscience, and *"religious beliefs?"*

Are churches and Private Christian Schools, specifically organized for the purpose of disseminating the gospel message of Jesus Christ, also guilty of discrimination and *"hate crimes"* for refusing to hire individuals who choose alternative lifestyles, such as *adultery, fornication,* or *homosexuality?*

Government Coercion and Censorship

By reclassifying select Bible passages as *"hate speech"* and by mandating Christian pastors and leaders to perform *"same-sex weddings"* under the threat of *"fines or imprisonment,"* places judges and politicians which legislate those decrees in a position of allegedly committing *"coercion,"* which is a *felony*, and *"censorship."*

According to the ACLU, "Censorship, the suppression of words, images, or ideas that are 'offensive,' happens whenever some people succeed in imposing their personal, political, or moral values on others. Censorship can be carried out by the government as well as private pressure groups. Once you allow the government to censor someone else, you cede to it the power to censor you, or something you like. Censorship is like poison gas: A powerful weapon that can harm you when the wind shifts. Censorship by the government is unconstitutional because freedom of speech is protected in the first amendment, and is guaranteed to all Americans."

The Supreme Court has interpreted the First Amendment's protection of free speech and artistic expressions very broadly extending to books, theatrical works and paintings, posters, television, music videos, comic books – literally to whatever creativity the human mind produces.

Historically, those who demand rights for *"alternative lifestyle"* choices are the groups and individuals who use *"coercion," "censorship,"* and *"reclassification ideologies"* in an attempt to force their views upon individuals who cherish *"traditional values"* (Judges 19:22-25). Not vice versa!

We Must Obey God, Not Man
Proclaiming the gospel message of freedom from sin through the shed blood of Jesus Christ no longer becomes possible if government *"organizes religion,"* by telling us what portions of the Bible we are allowed to agree with and teach, and forbids

Christians to talk about all the behavioral choices listed in the Bible, as sins, from which mankind is in need of forgiveness and redemption.

Any government which censors the *"independent thinking"* and *"free speech"* of its citizens by reclassifying portions of the Bible that call homosexuality a sin, as, *"hate words"* or *"hate speech,"* and prosecutes those who teach or verbalize a belief in those Scriptures with committing malicious *"hate crimes,"* has become a *"tyranny"* that must resolutely be resisted. At this point, Christians must purposefully obey God, not man.

We Must Stand Firm Now
When faced with persecution from various activist groups and politicians, Paul firmly stood on his legal rights as a Roman citizen.

> *25 As they stretched him out to flog him, Paul said to the centurion standing there, "Is it legal for you to flog a Roman citizen who hasn't even been found guilty?"*
> *26 When the centurion heard this, he went to the commander and reported it. "What are you going to do?" he asked. "This man is a Roman citizen."*
> *27 The commander went to Paul and asked, "Tell me, are you a Roman citizen?" "Yes, I am," he answered.*
> *28 Then the commander said, "I had to pay a lot of money for my citizenship." "But I was born a citizen," Paul replied.*
>
> Acts 22:25-28 NIV

Freedom Is Never Free

As free-born citizens of the United States of America, we must fight hard, now, for our Constitution and its First Amendment Rights to *"Freedom of Speech"* and *"Religious Liberty."* The failure to decisively choose to stand firmly, now, will result in the loss of everything our nation's founders fought so hard to ensure.

We Must Draw a Line in the Sand
We have grown up with freedoms that citizens in other nations have never known. Having judges, political officials, or *"the Gestapo"* tell us what we are allowed to read, believe, and publicly proclaim, has never been a part of our lives. The very idea that, our great nation could actually be overrun by tyranny and a political ideology that no longer makes room for *"free speech"* and *"religious liberty,"* is foreign to most Americans.

Wake up! We are just years away from losing all of the God given freedoms we have enjoyed because our forefathers had the foresight to draft a Constitution and advance a *"limited government"* that restrains the inherent wickedness of all its leaders through employing a separation of governing powers philosophy, that allows every American to passionately chase their personal dreams of life, liberty, and the pursuit of happiness, without government interference.

Respect and honor should be shown to those holding any office or position of authority. But when the apostles were told they could no longer teach in the name of Jesus, Peter and John replied, *"Which is right in God's eyes: to listen to you, or to Him? You be the judges! As for us, we cannot help speaking about what we have seen and heard" (Acts 4:19-20 NIV).*

A government that tells its citizens what portions of the Bible they are allowed to publicly read, believe, and preach must respectfully be ignored. We must obey God, not man!

National Religious Liberty Day

As pastors and Christian leaders, we might be wise to consider banding together, cross-denominationally, and proclaiming a *National Religious Liberty Day*. This special *day of freedom,* if celebrated on a Sunday with nationwide participation, would facilitate the optimum effect and result.

On *National Religious Liberty Day*, every participating minister will boldly take a stand for our Constitutional right to *"free speech"* and *"religious freedom,"* by courageously proclaiming, from every pulpit in America, our right and intention to read, teach, and preach from any Scripture in the Bible we wish to address, including portions of texts that refer to *adultery, fornication, and homosexuality as sins.* Every participating pastor and leader would then recite Romans 1:18-32 and read a statement similar to the following example.

> *"In no way do I advocate discrimination, hatred, rejection, or violence against any human being, including homosexuals. However, I completely agree with the Scripture passages that I just read in support of the Biblical view of sexual, marital, and family values."*

Prepare for a Battle

Those who insist on their own way and oppose *"free speech"* and *"religious liberty,"* will not just lie down and quit. There will be many lawsuits, lines that we must draw in the sand, and

Freedom Is Never Free

very expensive legal battles that we must be willing to sacrifice for, fight, and win.

This is the time that all of us as pastors and Christian leaders must lay aside our minor doctrinal differences, pool our finances into a *"common legal defense fund,"* and stand united in support of our Constitutional rights to *"free speech"* and *"religious liberties"* for all. The American Center for Law and Justice, (www.aclj.org), founded by Jay Sekulow, is a legal defense organization with a proven track record of excellence that the author of this book recommends supporting.

In the words of the 40th President of the United States of America, Ronald Reagan,

> *"Freedom is never more than one generation away from extinction. We didn't pass it to our children in the bloodstream. It must be fought for, protected, and handed on for them to do the same, or one day we will spend our sunset years telling our children and our children's children what it was once like in the United States where men were free."*

Freedom is never free!

Chapter Eleven
The Face of Genuine Revival

I remember the vision I had in 1993 as if it took place yesterday. Raging fires were burning and consuming every major city in the United States of America as rioting, looting, terrorism, and mayhem filled the streets. Like *"houses of cards,"* the financial markets fell thousands of points in one day. Due to the sudden collapse of the U.S. Dollar, Americans stormed their banks in a futile attempt to withdraw money that was no longer available. With the most prestigious Financial Investment Firms in the world brought to their knees by such a swift, sudden collapse, that everyone, including Christians, believed to be impossible; panic set in, and China overtook America as the world's new superpower.

With our nation's power grids failing, coast to coast, as a result of high-tech, Islamic jihadists (trained at our universities), hacking into the command and control computer systems of America's infrastructure, our president was forced to dispatch the National Guard and declare Martial Law.

I remember weeping without control as the Lord's voice so clearly resonated within my spirit, *"Unless genuine revival returns to the United States, everything you just saw in this vision will happen in America."* But, just what is "genuine revival?"

Does Anyone Care?

I feel like a lone voice screaming in the middle of the desert, trying to warn God's people and America of a certain fiery apocalypse looming on the horizon to consume our prosperity, leaving only small piles of ashes as mere reminders of what our country once was, and previously enjoyed.

I believe we may be just years away from similar, chaotic events unfolding in every one of our cities, coast to coast. With a national debt approaching $20 trillion, and an inability to pay our bills, the Feds just continue to print more money as if we are all taking our turn to roll the dice while playing a nationwide game of Monopoly. If the train Americans are riding is not halted, all of us shall lose in the real game of life as Boardwalk and Park Place are reduced to ashes along with the rest of our great American cities.

With an urgency I've never had in my entire life, I'm frantically trying to warn America and God's people. And yet, very few seem interested in listening. Even some pastors, leaders, and Christians want to pretend all of this will just go away and that consequences no longer exist for sin and moral decay.

We Have Ears But No Longer Hear

I had just finished speaking in one of our nation's great churches about a need for *"genuine revival."* While exiting the building, a young man approached me and commented, "You are so right

Rev. Wetteland. Our nation is falling apart and we must have revival. We desperately need God to do something!"

I did not even think. I just reacted. Turning around, I boldly responded,

> *"Did you not hear a word I said? Were you not listening? America is collapsing because our churches have become rest homes for the disobedient! We don't need God to do something! God needs us to do something! We need to obey Christ!"*

Obedient Leadership Fosters Revival

"Genuine Revival" occurs when we, as pastors and leaders, pave the way forward by allowing God the freedom to change our hardened hearts so we become uncomfortable with ourselves and the way we currently are living our Christian lives, and leading our church congregations. How we pastor our churches and lead God's flock comprises the most important *"keys"* to *"genuine revival!"*

When we, as shepherds of Christ's flock, become grieved with our self-centered budgets, *"internally"* directed over spending (see chapter 7 on page 57), sanctimonious castles that we have built in the sand, and decide to serve Christ instead of ourselves; *"genuine revival,"* then, becomes possible.

Instead of obeying Christ and being *"Leaders Who Lead,"* we have been *"independent contractors,"* fiercely competing with one another and striving to build our own, nonexistent empires. When we reach the end of ourselves and can no longer live with our hypocrisy, we will be unable to continue doing church, *"as usual."* With sincere repentance, we will seek God, fall on the Rock (Jesus), and ask the King of the Universe to search our hearts, forgive our disobedience, and grant His mercy so we may truly be *"Leaders Who Lead."*

With repentant hearts and a renewed passion to go after the lost and care for the poor, we shall instruct our church boards to refocus spending outwardly to assist the downcast and unfortunate who live amongst us. As true, Christ-centered shepherds, we will courageously organize and spearhead teams of servants charging into our community's darkest neighborhoods so we may be the *"real"* Jesus and *Feed* those who are hungry, give a *Drink* to the thirsty, provide *Shelter* for the homeless, *Clothe* those who are naked, *Care* for the sick, and *Visit* those who are in prison.

This is the type of *"Leadership Which Leads,"* and fosters *"genuine revival!"* Pastors and leaders who shepherd God's flock in this manner will be those who are seated at Christ's right hand when He says:

> *34 ...Come, you who are blessed by my Father; take your inheritance, the kingdom prepared for you since the creation of the world.*
> *35 For I was hungry and you gave me something to eat, I was thirsty and you gave me something to drink, I was a stranger and you invited me in,*
> *36 I needed clothes and you clothed me, I was sick and you looked after me, I was in prison and you came to visit me."*

Matthew 25:34-36 NIV

The Marketers and Utter Stupidity

Much of what we have termed *"revival"* in America, at best, have been nothing more than exciting services filled with great preaching, shouting, laughter, and emotion that we then market and sell as the latest revival music, revival T-shirts, revival coffee cups, and *How to Have a Revival* books, so we may promote our meeting, receive notoriety, and become wealthy.

How can we lead, and attend church services regularly, walk right past the poor and neediest people in our communities, and do absolutely nothing to assist with their daily essentials? And, then, because we happen to have a few exciting church services with lots of tears, emotion, and energy, we claim that we are in a *"revival."*

Afterwards, we head right back into another church service to sing, dance, and shout *"praise the Lord,"* only to leave that meeting as we pass a homeless mother and her children on the way to a restaurant to consume our 4th meal of the day so we may chat with our Christian friends about how richly and wonderfully God was moving in the *"revival"* service. Jesus must weep at such utter nonsense.

Christ-Centered Leadership Required

Until the truth sinks in deep enough, and hurts bad enough, so that we as pastors and leaders face our disobedience, obey Christ, change the way that we disburse funds, *"do church,"* and begin to mobilize our congregations to practically serve the lost and hurting people living in our communities; we really are not free at all (John 8:31-32). We have only embraced an alternate form of deception, with which we console ourselves and our parishioners, by falsely inferring that everything is okay if we just attend church and pray.

Have we never understood that Jesus was speaking to the pastors and leaders of the Laodicea-type of churches when He rebuked the lukewarm, self-indulgent leaders, saying, *"...I will spit you out of My mouth"? (Revelation 3:16 NIV).*

A Byproduct of Godly Leadership

"Genuine Revival" is a natural byproduct of *"Leaders Who Lead"* their church congregations to obey Christ and to serve their immediate, communities' needs by aggressively going after the lost and feeding Jesus when He is hungry, giving Him a drink when He is thirsty, inviting Him into our homes when He is homeless, clothing Him when He is naked, caring for Him when He is sick, and visiting Him when He is in prison.

Why is this true? This is because Jesus said, *"Truly I tell you, whatever you did for one of the least of these brothers and sisters of Mine, you did for Me" (Matthew 25:40 NIV).*

This is so clear! When we as pastors and leaders build *"team leadership"* structures into our congregations to fish for those who are lost by serving our community's needs and caring for the poor; we are *"doing this unto Jesus,"* and honoring Him so our obedience fosters *"genuine revival."*

But, when we, as pastors and leaders, fail to take the lead and shepherd our congregations to go after those who are lost by not serving the needs of people in our immediate communities and refusing to care *"for the least of these, Christ's brethren amongst us,"* we have chosen to not do this to Jesus and have, thus, publicly dishonored Christ and have announced to the world why *"genuine revival"* will never visit the doorstep of our assemblies.

Godly Pastors, the Key to Revival

The prophet, Jeremiah, provides us with a snapshot of *"genuine revival,"* which occurs as a result of pastors who shepherd their congregations according to God's directives.

> *15 "Then I will give you shepherds after my own heart, who will lead you with knowledge and understanding.*
>
> *16 In those days, when your numbers have increased greatly in the land," declares the Lord, "people will no longer say, 'The Ark of the covenant of the Lord.' It will never enter their minds or be remembered; it will not be missed, nor will another one be made.*
>
> *17 At that time they will call Jerusalem The throne of the Lord, and all nations will gather in Jerusalem to honor the name of the Lord. No longer will they follow the stubbornness of their evil hearts."*

Jeremiah 3:15-17 NIV

The heart of God is for pastors and leaders to shepherd their congregations into selflessly reaching out to the lost in their communities and feeding Jesus when He is hungry, giving Him a drink when He is thirsty, inviting Him into our homes when He is homeless, clothing Him when He is naked, caring for Him when He is sick, and visiting Him when He is in prison.

When we, as pastors and leaders, obey Christ and shepherd God's flock in this manner, our self-centered stubbornness will leave. From the pastors to the parishioners, our hearts will be broken with a passion to search for the lost, share Christ in our neighborhoods, feed the poor, and care for the needy. *"Genuine Revival,"* will then be fostered, and the number of people in our church congregations, according to Jeremiah, will be *"increased greatly!"* Not for the purpose that we may receive notoriety, but so that Christ, alone, may be glorified!

"Genuine Revival" is the fruit of godly pastors who, as *"Leaders Who Lead,"* shepherd their congregations into selflessly laying down their lives, as a team, to go out and get the lost, and to serve the needs and neediest people, in their communities.

Self-Centered Pastors Will Be Removed

Without *"genuine revival,"* America has no chance of survival. The freedoms our founding fathers fought to provide for all of us to enjoy will all be lost in the blink of an eye, if we as pastors, leaders, and believers, don't obey Christ's commands now.

Our nation can only change as people change. God, alone, has the ability to transform the hardened hearts of hard-working dads, moms, teenagers, community leaders, and politicians. But we are partners with the work God does in other people through *"obedience."* We must take Jesus into the workplace, and our communities, through the persistence of, personally, going out to search for the lost, serve the needy, care for the poor, and bring them in. This is *"hard work,"* which is the essence of *"genuine revival."* Revival is not a *"service"* that we attend, revival is the *"serving"* that we do.

Far, too, many of us, as pastors and leaders have been telling our congregations that, in order for *"revival"* to come we just need to pray more. So, we hide behind the four walls of our elaborate sanctuaries and cry out to God with our *"sin filled"* prayers of imploring Christ to do what we refuse to do, asking Him to draw people to our churches, while we disobey His commands to *"go out and get them."* Then, while we down numerous cups of coffee and consume dozens of donuts, we piously console ourselves by telling one another how powerful our prayer meetings are, and how Jesus surely was present.

No, Christ doesn't participate in those types of prayer meetings. While we were drinking coffee, eating donuts, and calling our disobedience, *"prayer,"* Jesus was holding the hungry child we neglected to feed. He was comforting the single mom we refused to help. And He was thanking, and saluting the homeless Vietnam Veteran Hero, whom we just scorned with our comment of *"...why don't you get a real job and work for a change?"*

Possibly, do you think, if we feed Christ when He is hungry, give Him a drink when He is thirsty, invite Him into our homes when He is homeless, clothe Him when He is naked, care for Him when He is sick, and visit Him when He is in prison, that just, maybe, we actually will start leading people to Christ, and, *"revival,"* instead of a menacing apocalypse to blanket the cities of America?

This, however, will never happen until we, as pastors and leaders, purposely choose to possess the heart of Christ and fearlessly lead our church congregations to selflessly fish for the lost by serving the needs, and neediest people, in our communities.

For this very reason, Ezekiel thundered!

> ...*This is what the Sovereign Lord says: Woe to you shepherds of Israel who only take care of yourselves! ...You have not strengthened the weak or healed the sick or bound up the injured. You have not brought back the strays or searched for the lost....I am against the shepherds and will hold them accountable...I will remove them from attending the flock so that the shepherds can no longer feed themselves.*
>
> Ezekiel 34:2, 4, 10 NIV

What Is Genuine Revival?

What is *"genuine revival?"* If ten people were asked this question, ten different answers would be given. If, however, we were to ask Jesus this question, I believe He would have one clear answer.

"Genuine Revival" is Christ's response to our obedience. When we, as pastors and leaders, direct our church congregations to go after the lost by serving the needs of our communities and *Feeding* Jesus when He is hungry, giving Him a *Drink* when He is thirsty, *Inviting* Christ in our homes when He is homeless, *Clothing* Him when He is naked, *Caring* for Jesus when He is sick, and *Visiting* Him when He is in prison – Christ will then show up in our church services and the Holy Spirit will flow to initiate repentance, save the lost, heal the sick, restore the brokenhearted, change our hard calloused hearts, and set the captives free.

The Face of Genuine Revival

Revival music, revival T-shirts, revival coffee cups, and *How to Have a Revival* books, will not be marketed and sold to bring attention to a special speaker, to ourselves, or for the purpose of becoming wealthy.

A pastor, or a leader, will simply give thanks to God for His goodness, dismiss the service, and send the believers back into their communities to go after the lost and *Feed* Jesus when He is hungry, give Him a *Drink* when He is thirsty, *Invite* Him into our homes when He is homeless, *Clothe* Him when He is naked, *Care* for Him when He is sick, and *Visit* Him when He is in prison. No one will try to seize credit, or receive notoriety, as a benefit from God moving in our midst.

And we keep on serving, and serving, and serving... This is what pleases Christ and will save ourselves, and America, from a certain fiery apocalypse. This is the face of *"genuine revival!"*

Revival Truths from This Chapter

- America is collapsing because our churches have become rest homes for the disobedient.

- We don't need God to do something! God needs us to do something! We need to obey Christ!

- How we pastor our churches and lead God's flock comprises the most important *"keys"* to *"genuine revival."*

- *"Genuine Revival"* is a natural byproduct of *"Leaders Who Lead"* their church congregations to obey Christ and to serve their immediate community's needs by aggressively going after the lost and feeding Jesus when

He is hungry, giving Him a drink when He is thirsty, inviting Him into our homes when He is homeless, clothing Him when He is naked, caring for Him when He is sick, and visiting Him when He is in prison.

- With repentant hearts and a renewed passion to go after the lost and care for the poor, we shall instruct our church boards to refocus spending outwardly to assist the downcast and unfortunate who live amongst us.

- Our nation can only change as people change. God, alone, has the ability to transform the hardened hearts of hard-working dads, moms, teenagers, community leaders, and politicians. But we are partners with the work God does in other people through *"obedience."*

- Revival is not a *"service"* that we attend, revival is the *"serving"* that we do.

- *"Genuine Revival"* is Christ's response to our obedience.

- Revival music, revival T-shirts, revival coffee cups, and *How to Have a Revival* books, will not be marketed and sold to bring attention to a special speaker, to ourselves, or for the purpose of becoming wealthy.

- No one will try to seize credit, or to receive notoriety, as a benefit from God moving in our midst.

Chapter Twelve
Share Your Story

On a beautiful, July evening in Oswego, Illinois, I stopped at a local Starbucks for a cappuccino. The sun was just beginning to set and the temperature was still a very steamy 82°. With several movie theaters nearby, and numerous restaurants and shops, quite a number of college kids, and adults, were outdoors enjoying the warm weather and drinking coffee.

While entering Starbucks, I noticed two college-aged girls sitting at an outdoor table to my left, staring at me. The Holy Spirit quickly nudged my heart and I knew this was a divine appointment.

We All Have a Story to Share
Every one of us has a story, something simple, supernatural, or miraculous that Christ has done in our lives. Our stories are the most relatable and effective tools, for leading other people to Jesus, that we possess.

Nothing else is needed. A degree in theology or a special class in public speaking is unnecessary because, our stories are more than adequate. We may share the chronicles of our lives, confidently, with everyone.

The Holy Spirit Draws People to Us

After purchasing my cappuccino, I walked out of the Starbucks and headed for the outdoor table occupied by the two college girls that were still glancing in my direction.

You see, I have learned to recognize signs that indicate the Holy Spirit is at work, drawing other people to us, so we may lead them to Jesus. The following behaviors are just a few examples: When complete strangers stare at us, ask us questions, move closer to us, sigh, glance at us, talk to themselves, show an interest in something we own or are wearing, fidgeting, or, when an individual is very talkative.

Have You Heard My Story?

Casually, I approached the two young ladies, and introduced myself. "Hi girls, I am Kim. Have you ever heard my story?"

Of course they have never heard my story. I realize this. However, I have introduced myself to hundreds of people in this manner, to quickly break the ice and to open a door to share my testimony. This is easily accomplished by anyone. The next time you are in a grocery store, or are out in public and someone glances at you, smile, and just ask, "Have you heard my story?"

The young woman with brown hair said, "How could I possibly have heard your story? I have never met you." "Well, do you mind if I share it with you?" I replied. "Sure, why not. We're not going anywhere and we've got all night."

Share Your Story

In today's society, people are very busy and often do not have a lot of time. In order to be sensitive to hectic schedules, I have learned to share my story in 60 seconds, if that is all the time an individual has available.

I Should Not Be Alive
After finding out each girl's name, and the local technical college they attended, I took a seat at their table and made sure that my body language, and my demeanor, was relaxed, warm, and friendly. Then, I began talking as if all of us have been friends for years; making sure that I smiled often, and made direct, but non-confrontational, eye contact.

"Jennifer, Carrie, I shouldn't be alive today, enjoying this cappuccino, and talking with you girls. At the age of 15, I was very ill with a rare form of salmonella food poisoning that was genetically similar to typhoid fever. I spent two weeks at Copley Memorial Hospital, just down the street in Aurora, with a fever of 108°. At one point during my hospital stay, I actually died, and a team of medical professionals had to restart my heart.

When the crisis was finally over, Dr. Newman, a Jewish cardiologist sat on the edge of my bed and broke the news – my heart had been severely damaged and I would not live to see the age of 29! I was crushed, didn't know what to do, and thought my life was over.

The next day, my father who was a World War II Veteran, entered my room and bluntly said, 'Maybe if you quit feeling sorry for yourself and pray for other people whose prognosis is worse than your condition, maybe God will heal you.' I was so angry! I mean, why would my dad say such a thing? He was not even a Christian, and rarely, went to church.

After thinking about what my father had said, I called the head nurse and requested a list of people's names, whose conditions were terminal, so I could pray for them. Girls, I will never forget looking at that list, because, I didn't even know how to pray. I simply said, 'God, please help these people whose conditions are worse than mine.' Suddenly, this tremendous peace came all over me and I fell asleep. At the time, I did not realize the peace that I felt, actually, was the presence, and healing power, of Jesus Christ.

The following day a nurse took an electrocardiogram test on my heart at 6 AM. She returned to conduct additional EKGs at 10 AM, and again at noon. Thinking that my condition was worsening, I inquired several times, as to why all of these tests were being repeated. No one gave me an answer.

At 2 PM, Dr. Newman finally arrived and his appearance was quite pale. He showed me the test results from seven, previous EKGs that corroborated severe damage in my heart. Dr. Newman then displayed the strips of cardiac tape from the three EKGs taken that morning. Documented, medical evidence from those EKGs revealed that the previously confirmed damage to my heart was mysteriously gone. Jesus healed me!"

The Gods of Egypt

Carrie looked at me with such a sweet smile, and added her thoughts. "That's great! Jennifer and I are really happy that happened for you, but we are not Christians, and we don't

Share Your Story

believe the way that you do." "Oh, so what do you girls believe?" I inquired. With such a convincing tone in her voice, Carrie looked directly into my eyes, and said, "We believe in the gods of Egypt."

Having thought that I, about, had heard everything, for a moment, I was so taken back, that I nearly said, "Wow! Your story sounds more interesting than mine. Let me hear what you have to say?"

Quickly, I gathered myself and began to share various passages of Scripture with, both, Carrie and Jennifer. "Kim," Carrie interrupted, "We don't believe the Bible so you might as well stop trying to share anything with us from that book."

Without the Holy Spirit's guidance, I would not have known what to do. The key, needed, to open the hearts of Carrie and Jennifer was simple. Looking at both girls, I asked, "If Jesus, personally, revealed Himself to you, so that you know He died on the cross for your sins, rose from the dead, still lives today as your personal Savior, and that He is alive and real, would you believe in Him?"

To my astonishment, Jennifer quickly replied, "Well of course we would! Why wouldn't we? I mean, if Jesus revealed Himself to us then we would know He is real. Of course we would believe!"

Pray Publicly With People
Here is where many make a huge mistake. Instead of praying with an individual right then and there, in public, we completely

turn our backs on God, and the person we are talking to, and say, "I'll keep you in prayer." And then we walk away.

Without any hesitation, I extended my hands to Jennifer and Carrie, and said, "Let's pray." With folded arms, both of the girls just glared at me and did nothing. So I said, "What's the problem? Are you afraid all your friends are going to see you holding hands with a preacher?"

"No, that's not it at all," Carrie exclaimed. "We have had lots of people, just like you, talk to us about Jesus. But none of them have ever prayed with us. I mean, some have said they would pray for us, but no one actually prayed with us like you want to."

Finally, Jennifer and Carrie unfolded their arms and each of them held one of my hands. Then, I asked Jesus to, personally, reveal Himself to these precious, beautiful, girls. After praying, I wrote my cell phone number down on the jacket of a Starbucks cup, gave it to Carrie, and told both of the girls to call me if they ever needed anything.

As I walked away, Jennifer said, "Kim, do you think Jesus will reveal Himself to us?" Turning around, and with a smile on my face, I said, "Absolutely! And if He does not, then Christ does not exist and you should never worship Him!" I could not believe I was that bold, however, Jesus clearly said that He will never deny Himself (2 Timothy 2:13).

The Phone Call

Several months later, my cell phone rang at 3 o'clock in the morning. "Who in the world would be calling me at this time of the night?" I thought. I noticed the call was coming from the

Chicago area, but I did not recognize the number. My wife told me that someone might have a need and urged me to answer my phone.

On the other end of the line was the sweet-sounding voice of a young female. "Do I know you?" I inquired. "My friend and I spoke to you at a Starbucks. Do you remember us?" she replied. Since I visit Starbucks frequently, and talk to lots of people, I could not recall who this girl was – especially at 3 AM. "Do you remember the two girls who worshiped the gods of Egypt?" she asked. I almost wanted to say, "How could I ever forget that? We nearly could have made a movie over that cup of coffee!"

"Well, this is Carrie and Jennifer, and we wanted you to know that Jesus just revealed Himself to us. We are at a Christian coffeehouse with friends and just surrendered our lives to Christ. You took the time to care, and to pray with us, and we wanted to let you know that we are now, Christians."

Share Your Story

I have numerous examples, similar to Jennifer and Carrie's conversions, as a result of obeying the Holy Spirit's prompting to ask complete strangers a simple question, "Have you heard my story?"

Sharing our stories with other people is a simple, easy way for all of us to change America from the grassroots level, one person at a time. Your story is the testimony of what Jesus Christ has personally done for you. No one knows your story better than you. Practice your method of delivery in front of a mirror, and with your friends. Refine your presentation so you can share your story in as little as, one minute, if necessary.

Then, choose to make a difference and be a part of helping to save, and change, America's future. The next time you are out in public and notice that someone is glancing in your direction, smile, walk up to that person and inquire, "Hey, have you heard my story?" Soon, you will be praying with that individual to surrender their life to Christ and you will be helping to change our nation, one person at a time.

Chapter Thirteen
Covert Affairs

A *covert operation* (also known as *CoveOps* or *covert ops*), "is an operation that is so planned and executed as to conceal the identity of or to permit plausible denial by the sponsor." The intent of such a mission is to create a political and or business implication which may facilitate the planned, objective outcomes from a *"spillover effect"* of its implementation, in the military, intelligence or law-enforcement arenas, and ultimately, into society. Covert operations aim to fulfill their mission objectives without any parties knowing who championed or carried out the operation, or having insight into what the mission objectives were or how, and if, they actually were achieved. Ultimately, only the sponsor knows if the mission was successful. In essence, this is a *"covert operation."*

The Mission Objectives
Having the foresight and ingenuity of how today's, modern societies function, Jesus authored the greatest *"covert operations"* mission in history. In the Parable of the Ten Minas, Christ called ten of His servants *"...gave them ten minas, and*

said to them, 'Engage in business until I come' (Luke 19:13 ESV).

According to Thayer's Greek Lexicon, *pragmateuomai*, the Greek word translated as, "engage in business," means, "to be occupied in anything, to carry on a business, or to carry on the business of a banker or a trader."

Jesus commanded us to utilize our intelligence, to become highly skilled and educated, and to *"covertly"* infiltrate every aspect of modern society by functioning under cover as hard-working CEOs, managers, and employees in order to accomplish the planned objectives – to influence and convert every person to Christ, within the public, private, and geopolitical arenas of commerce and government.

A Real Life Covert Operation

I was preaching a message regarding the application of a *"covert mission"* in Ajax, Ontario Canada. After the service a young man named Alex, was filled with enthusiasm and ran to the platform, shouting, "Rev. Wetteland, you gave me the answer! You gave me the answer!"

A year later, I was invited to speak at this church again and Alex told me his story. Upon graduation from college Alex landed a great position with an International Tech Distribution Company at one of the branches located near Toronto. Sensing God's direction to function in management, Alex was heading nowhere in life, that is, until he understood Christ's perspective on the subject of *"Covert Operations."*

Alex arrived early to work on Monday. Hired as an average, regular employee, he was overflowing with excitement and armed with a *"covert"* plan. With a warm smile on his face, and an abundance of passion, he greeted all fifteen of his coworkers, and purposely spoke something to inspire each individual.

During the next few months Alex methodically retrieved the birthdays, anniversaries, and special days that were important to each person. Detailed files were kept to highlight the preferences, likes and dislikes, number of children, pets, hobbies, and personal goals of each employee. Alex entered the birthdays of all fifteen coworkers, along with those of their spouses and children, plus, anniversaries and other significant dates, into his smart phone and tagged each event with an alarm. When reminded of a birthday or special event for a fellow employee, their spouse or a child, Alex would purchase a greeting card to demonstrate his gratitude and appreciation. Often, he also would include a gift card to a local restaurant.

Alex consistently followed this protocol. Like clockwork, daily, he would greet all fifteen coworkers with a smile and an encouraging word, like, "So good to see you! I sure appreciate you!" or, "I learn so much from you!" Alex remembered every birthday and even went to several ball games to support events that were important to their children.

The Promotion
One day, Alex was summoned to meet with his boss and several company executives from the corporate office. "Alex," conveyed his boss, "out of all the company's outlets, across Canada, I am sure you are aware that our branch has been number one in every area of performance and quality control, for

the past year. A research team has been conducting an investigation to determine why, our branch, has been outperforming all company affiliates in Canada. The findings of their study have concluded that your excellence in job performance and leadership skills are the reason for the outstanding success of our branch. Congratulations, you are the new branch manager." Alex's salary package, plus benefits, nearly doubled!

Our Serving, Not Our Sermons
Hard work and serving are the vital keys necessary for the success of any *"covert operation."* As mentioned earlier in this book, people do not listen to our *"sermons,"* they listen to our *"serving."*

Alex's willingness to serve, assist, and encourage everyone, not only captured the attention of his immediate supervisor, which resulted in a promotion, but also won him the respect and cooperation of all his coworkers. Everyone at that branch works their butts off for Alex.

Anytime someone has a personal or family need, Alex shows up at their home to help. After working at this tech firm for a little over one year, nearly half of all the employees that Alex, now supervises, attend the church cell group meetings held at his home and have surrendered their lives to Christ.

To this day, Alex's immediate supervisor, along with the company's owner, have no clue that a *"covert operation"* is being conducted, right under their noses, to lead all of their employees to Christ. No one ever sees Alex preaching *"sermons,"* they only see him helping and *"serving,"* – and this makes everyone happy. And yet, the *"serving"* that Alex does at work is the *"key"* that unlocks the hearts of his coworkers to receive Christ when he shows up at their home to help with a family need.

The mission objectives, to lead every employee to Christ at that tech firm, are being carried out without anyone knowing the sponsor's identity or that such an undertaking even exists, and has been deployed with complete, ongoing success. This is a true *"covert operation."*

Covert Ops for Every Church

Every local church would benefit greatly from having a *Covert Operations Plan* and a highly skilled Covert Ops Director.

A Covert Ops Director would conduct regular surveys of the church family to determine where each church member is employed within a local community. With this information, the Director, along with an Examination Committee, would seek the Lord's guidance to determine which local businesses to target for the deployment of a *"covert operations"* plan.

Every business or company that employs a church member is a potential target for a well-organized *"covert mission."* However, only those companies that employ church members who have passed a well thought out, *Covert Ops Training School* should be considered.

Covert Ops Training School

"Covert Ops" is a serious, committed local missions plan to convert every employee to Christ at a local business or company, within a community. This is not a game and only serious

candidates, capable of following the mission objectives should apply.

Approved candidates would be trained in the following areas.

- Commitment
- Integrity with God
- Real Christianity
- Loving People
- Relationship with God
- Your Serving Is Everything
- Practical Serving
- Integrity at Work
- Integrity of the Mission
- Influencing Your Supervisors
- Influencing Your Coworkers
- Collecting and Recording Personal Data
- Going the Extra Mile
- How to Share Your Story
- How to Pray With People
- How to Lead People to Jesus
- How to Bring Someone to Church

Upon graduation from the above *Covert Ops Training Classes*, each approved candidate would then be evaluated for deployment into their secular environment by the Covert Ops Director and the Examination Committee.

Changing America's Future

"Covert Ops" is a serious training program and plan to change the moral structure and fabric of America via the deployment of

a *"covert operation"* strategically implemented with *"mission objectives"* to convert thousands of people to Christ through *"serving"* our supervisors and coworkers, within and outside, the workplace environment.

This is not a game. Commitment, training, and a lot of hard work are required from every pastor, leader, and parishioner in America. As a nation, we are in the final stages of moral decay, which historically, in every previous great Empire, has ended in the ashes and ruins of total collapse.

America is in desperate need of revival. But, revival is not a *"service"* that we attend, revival is the *"serving"* that we do, and is Christ's response to our *"obedience."*

We can all sit around and pretend that America really is not in trouble and that things will improve as long as we persist to hide behind the walls of our elaborate sanctuaries, continue to do nothing, and just pray more. We can herald the vision from the father of our country, George Washington, as an entertaining novel which makes for good reading, scoff at David Wilkerson's vision of 1,000 fires burning in New York City alone, and ignore the contents of this book which may be God's final warning for America and the American Church.

Or, we can do something to save our nation from a certain apocalyptic end by obeying Christ's command to feed Jesus when He is hungry, give Him a drink when He is thirsty, invite Him into our homes when He is homeless, clothe Him when He is naked, care for Jesus when He is sick, and visit Him when He is in prison (Matthew 25:35-36).

The Coming American Apocalypse

The future of the United States of America rests in the balance of what you and I as pastors, leaders, parishioners, and citizens decide to do. The choice is ours. I truly believe this is America's Final Warning and the Church's Last Call.

Covert Ops Training Course

A *"Covert Ops"* training course, with a study workbook, is available on DVD for churches, Bible schools, Sunday schools, home Bible studies, and businesses. For information please contact Kim Wetteland Ministries at www.kimwettelandministries.com, or contact Pecan Grove Publishing at www.pecangrovepublishing.com.

Bulk Printed Book Orders

If you are interested in purchasing copies of this book in bulk for your church or ministry, please contact Pecan Grove Publishing through our site at www.pecangrovepublishing.com.